Pet HATES

The Shocking Truth about Pets and Vets

Josh Artmeier

ARGYLL✣PUBLISHING

© Josh Artmeier

First published 2006
Argyll Publishing
Glendaruel
Argyll PA22 3AE
Scotland
www.argyllpublishing.com

The author asserts his moral rights.

British Library Cataloguing-in-Publication Data.
A catalogue record for this book is available from
the British Library.

ISBN 1902831489

Printing: Mackays of Chatham

This book is dedicated to my parents,
my friends and the survivors.

Contents

Introduction

This book offers a uniquely honest – sometimes funny, sometimes sad and disturbing – picture of the life of a vet in the twenty first century. Make no mistake, be you a pet owner, a practising veterinary surgeon, a prospective or current student of veterinary science or nursing, *Pet Hates* will dramatically change your perspective on the profession.

In 2005 the suicide rate amongst vets in the UK hit the headlines: four times that of the population average, and twice that of doctors and nurses. I myself have worked in two practices where previous members of staff had killed themselves (in one of these two of them in fact!) and I have witnessed and heard of many vets breaking down under the stress of the job, drugs and alcohol being two of the common routes. Even during my veterinary studies one of my classmates repeatedly attempted to kill himself.[1]

New veterinary graduates can expect to be some £30,000 in debt but they cannot expect to immediately walk into a well-paid job. Yet so many people apparently want to be vets, and no one appears to understand or sympathise with those of us who, from time to time, find it a difficult way to earn a living. In fact, this is one of the main stress factors: there seems to be

---

[1] Go to 'A Typical Day' if you can't be bothered reading all this and want to get right into experiencing a vet's life!

a near-universal belief that it is a wonderful and rewarding calling and that anyone who doesn't find it so has something wrong with him or her and is undeserving of sympathy. It can be very difficult, then, to find anyone to talk to – hence the existence of the veterinary surgeons' helplines: + 44 (0) 1926 315119 and + 44 (0) 7659 811118.

I believe that the media (the plethora of books and 'reality' TV programmes on vetting) have a lot to answer for.[2] I hope this book will go some way towards correcting the balance, and ultimately, will save lives. With this as one of the book's major aims, I make no apologies for possibly shattering the illusions of those who idealise the profession. I have seen too much suffering to feel guilty about this.

Who is this book for?

1. Pet Owners This will give you some idea of what may lie behind the seemingly cheerful, caring and patient manner of your vet. Alternatively, when she or he appears not to be in the best of form, you might appreciate why. Particularly, this book should make you aware of the wide variety of attitudes that people have towards their animals, although we all start off assuming that everyone is like us. If your vet sometimes gets the approach wrong you will understand that this perhaps was the manner and attitude that suited the last client. Most of us are trying to do our best, but they don't teach mind-reading in vet school!

2. Those considering entering the profession Training to be a vet is a major commitment. Depend-

---

[2] Incidentally, according to a vet I know who appeared on one TV programme, these shows are often faked.

ing on where you study, it will take up to six years of very hard work, and at the end of this most of you will be heavily in debt. It is very hard to get an accurate idea of what being a vet is really like from school work experience or the odd weekend seeing practice, as everything appears new and exciting and you will generally be shielded from the most stressful aspects of the job. It is as well that you know what you are letting yourself in for before it is too late!

If, after reading this book, you are still determined to be a vet then you will be very well equipped to handle the vet school interview. Your detailed knowledge of what the job is really like will certainly impress your interviewers, who will know the score only too well. After all, they almost certainly opted for a life in academia after experiencing the sharp end!

3. Those studying to be vets and veterinary nurses
If you have only just embarked on your studies you might consider switching to something else, although admittedly it is very hard to relinquish a long-cherished dream. Failing that, you might start to make plans to move to one of the less stressful specialist areas. If these options are not feasible you will at least be in a very good position to ask the right questions of potential employers (and, I suggest, their employees) and so avoid some of the worst jobs. This book could save you a great deal of unpleasantness!

4. Recent graduates No, the problem isn't you! No, you are not alone! This book will be of great comfort if you are feeling isolated and depressed. It's very common for the thrill of graduation to give way rapidly to disillusion and depression, and to think there is something wrong with you. Well, many of us have been there, as you will see from this book, and there is a funny side to it!

5. Long-established vets and veterinary nurses
You should be familiar with much of this, and I think it'll raise a knowing chuckle or two. For some it may do you good to see the world through the eyes of a new graduate again. Bosses, this book might encourage you to treat your staff with more consideration!

Finally, readers should note that while there is an entry entitled Large Animal Work, this book concentrates on the small animal side of the profession. I have worked almost entirely as a small animal vet and, as farmers are increasingly struggling to make ends meet, large animal work is in decline and most graduates will spend most of their time dealing with pets.

Happy reading!

Josh Artmeier
Middlesex, England
July 2006

Abscesses

What better way to start this book than with the banal but important subject of abscesses? The glamorous and high-tech image of vets promoted by certain TV programmes would never lead you to suspect that abscesses are veterinary bread-and-butter, but a significant proportion of veterinary income depends on lancing, squeezing and flushing these pockets of pus.

The most commonly seen pus generator is the male domestic cat. These wretched creatures expend a high proportion of their energy attempting to rip each other to shreds, particularly if left unneutered. Typically the affected animal is presented 'with a broken leg', but the screams that issue from the frenzied febrile felid when you palpate the obvious lump give the game away. You clip the hair over the affected part, swab the site with disinfectant (more to impress the owner than anything else as one could hardly be importing more germs than are already partying away inside!), and slash it open with a blade. Usually the pussy puss objects to this and you may opt to perform the procedure in the absence of the owner,[1] often under sedation or anaesthetic.

---

[1] Personally I think it does owners good to witness the results of their folly (a) in having an unneutered cat – if indeed it is unneutered, (b) in letting it wander and terrorise other cats, and (c) in not bringing it along sooner.

A successful lancing is rewarded with a cascade of horribly foul-smelling, greenish pus, and sometimes a retching owner if he or she has chosen to be present. If the owner has not wanted the expense of anaesthetic then there is more struggling to follow while you flush the abscess with disinfectant. After that a quick shot of antibiotics, a homily on the virtues of early treatment if the brute's been in a fight, a packaging of tablets, a dismissal of the chastened owner, and a clean-up of the consulting room. (If you are feeling particularly peeved you can always dispense some disinfectant and suggest the owner flushes the wound daily.)

So, a large proportion of the veterinary day is devoted to expressing and mopping up assorted varieties of pus (and excrement). There are three main types of small animal pus: cat and dog pus (already satisfactorily described), guinea pig and rabbit pus, and reptile[2] and bird pus. Guinea pigs and rabbits are very prone to abscesses. These are often multiple and not easy to flush without anaesthetic as the white pus is extremely viscous and the animal almost impossible to hold. Birds and reptiles have the thickest and most intransigent pus of all. Squeezing the dried tooth-paste-like material is out of the question; you need to scrape out these abscesses with a curette, or administer general anaesthesia and remove the offending lumps *in toto*. Super.

---

[2] For reptiles see Exotics, p63

After-Hours Work

With great self-discipline you can remain smiley and bright from 9 am to 7 pm (normal working hours in many UK vet practices), at least on those days when there is time for a bite to eat and a cup of tea. It is difficult to maintain this saintly apprearance when called out of bed at 3 am to attend a so-called 'emergency'. True small animal emergencies are as rare as a Cavalier King Charles Spaniel (what a ridiculous name!) without anal gland problems.

Nine times out of ten the animal is either fine, or passably imitating a Norwegian Blue of Monty Python fame, and the vet's only task is to slip the bloodied corpse into a bodybag. Real emergencies are usually the upshot of days (or years) of folly or neglect on the part of the now hysterical owner, so it is hard to be sympathetic. Common examples would be the unvaccinated dog which has been spewing sewage-like substances from both ends for at least a day, [3] the dog attacked by a Rottweiler three days ago, now off its food and with a huge swelling on its neck, and the dog in severe respiratory distress, because the owner decided it wasn't necessary to replenish the tablets for heart failure as they seemed to have done the trick!

Road traffic accidents I would also class as preventable. Is it too much to expect people to keep their pets

see Parvovirus p117

on a lead? Visit any of the poorer areas of Britain and you'll see dogs of all sorts wandering at leisure across roads. Do people not realise that by letting their animals wander they are endangering the lives of children? (Dog in road, motorist swerves, dead kid!) I meditate on these matters when I am called out late at night to attend a dog with a broken leg or a cat with a smashed pelvis, but, somehow, I manage to hide my resentment, and return to bed seething and unable to sleep.

Anaesthesia

In my experience anaesthesia is the least standardised area of veterinary medicine, and new veterinary graduates in their first jobs will often find themselves forced to discard most of what they learnt at college and conform to the practice's own peculiar methods.

The first practice I worked for expected one to single-handedly administer intravenous anaesthetic to cats, and the boss only ever used thiopentone. He only employed male vets, and refused to employ nurses on the grounds that these were all women and that if he employed any then the vets and nurses would spend all their time flirting rather than getting on with the job – fat chance! He had also only just introduced a record system after insistence from his young assistants, and all surgical equipment was boiled up together in an open pan, from which one helped oneself to the instruments. I swear that this is true.

But back to the single-handed cat anaesthesia. Number one, it is not easy to get a cat to stay still while you're manipulating a rubber band around its leg and jabbing it with a needle. Number two, thiopentone is not only highly irritant if one misses the vein, but a slight overdose, if one's lucky enough to locate the target, would cause a cat to sleep until kingdom come! The younger vets at this practice, out of desperation or madness, had somehow come up with the idea that if one placed a rubber band over a cat's ears, the brute would hold still. It didn't work for me, and I have the scars to prove it.

Adopting the methods used by one's practice generally does make sense, primarily from the point of view of human relations. Can you imagine a new graduate waltzing into a practice and proclaiming that the method they have used 'successfully' for years (with only 'the occasional' anaesthetic death) is unacceptable? Also imagine the lack of support if something went wrong with any novel technique!

There's another use of thiopentone which I would not recommend. One of the many peculiar and seemingly inexplicable things I saw was its use with greyhounds. If you know anything about thiopentone, then you'll know that it's only short-acting by virtue of its redistribution into fat. In other words it's extremely long-acting in thin animals! One boss insisted on using it on these ultra-skinny dogs, and, as a result, they were never ready to go home in the evening, having to spend the night sleeping off the drug in the practice kennels, no doubt waking with massive hangovers the following day. I can only imagine that this had something to do with saving money by using this relatively cheap anaesthetic, and making more from the overnight stay!

Here are a couple of pet hates of mine regarding the practice of anaesthesia by vets:

(1) Anaesthetising geriatric animals without

checking kidney function or putting them on a drip. Often the poor creature dies miserably of kidney failure a few weeks later.

(2) Using drugs which drastically lower blood pressure, with the result that bleeders only become apparent when the animal wakes up. *Quelle horreur!*

(3) Anaesthetising small exotic animals. They need to be monitored very, very closely, and kept warm.

Anal Glands

Ah! The bane and the blessing of a vet's existence! How often do books and TV programmes fail to emphasise these wretched little diverticula, probably for fear of offending people whose main interest is schmaltzy anecdotes about puppies and calves. What a cop out! Anal glands are up there rivalling abscesses as major generators of veterinary income! It's almost enough to make you doubt the theory of evolution, that such an error-prone piece of anatomy could have come into being, but then dogs are selected by man and not nature.

You will have seen dogs savouring the olfactory delights of each other's posteriors? They are sniffing the scent produced by the anal glands. These are two sacs which open on the anal ring (yes, strictly speaking they should be called 'anal sacs'). They are situated at about half-past four, and half-past seven around the anus.[4] I lost all respect for an anatomy lecturer in veterinary college when she admitted she'd never squeezed an anal gland, and didn't know exactly where the openings were. Any practising veterinarian evacuates several every day, so you've got to know where they are!

Whenever an owner says he thinks the dog has

---

[4] By the way, civet anal gland secretions are used in perfume and known as musk.

worms because it's ('it's'? – well, most of them have been neutered!) been rubbing its backside on the carpet, the chances are the anal glands are full. The first thing you do is to request the owner to steady the head of his soon-to-be-struggling mutt. Most owners are totally incompetent at doing this, and so, for the umpteenth time that day you have to explain how to restrain the presently frantic Benji/Sheba or get up the courage to call a nurse. Then you put on a disposable glove, dip your index finger in a lubricant, and pop it into the anus, searching for a gland between your thumb and said sodomising forefinger. Usually a full gland is about the size of a grape, but it could be the size of a walnut, or so painful (ruptured) that there's no way you'll be able to feel it properly as the dog is doing bronco impersonations and the owner is distraught. In the latter case there will generally be a fistula – a hole from which blood, pus and anal secretion is leaking. You might try and flush it, but I usually check the other gland and then send the dog home on a course of antibiotics and pain killers, to be reviewed in a week or so. If the glands are not ruptured they will need squeezing. This can be easy or well-nigh impossible, depending on the consistency of the contents, the size of the opening and the degree of cooperation on the part of the dog and owner.

Cavalier King Charles Spaniel secretions are usually the consistency of smooth peanut butter and paler, many dogs produce watery black fluid with paler bits in it, and anything in between is possible. As a rule, I attempt to hold a piece of cotton wool over the glands as I squeeze them, at the same time trying to maintain a firm grip on the tail to anchor the writhing canid. This is not easy in docked Rottweilers – if you can manage them you must have a very strong nurse assisting you or you're Doctor-bloody-Doolittle!

It is not uncommon to receive a faceful of secretion as one squeezes, but it's worse when you can smell it somewhere on your person and can't locate the source.

Cats seldom suffer from anal gland problems but one occasion of persistent untraceable cat anal gland reek sticks in my mind. I was aware of secretion landing on my arms, but thought I'd scrubbed them adequately, and my nose couldn't find the concentrated source of the sick-making foetor anywhere as I drove back to the B&B after a hard day's locuming. I resolved to have a shower and then settle down to munch my sandwiches, free of animal smells, in front of the TV. It was only when I was thus ensconced and about to sink my teeth into my previously purchased provender, that I realised that all along the smell had been the brie cheese in my sandwiches! Hunger replaced disgust!

Antibiotics

No matter how principled you are as a veterinarian, you often find yourself giving way to the psychological pressure to over-prescribe antibiotics, for example to a cat with a very mild viral respiratory infection equivalent to a human cold. I'm tempted to say that people would never dream of visiting their doctors for such trivial afflictions, but I believe, in fact, that there are many idiots who do. Sometimes, when I am not feeling particularly rushed (seldom), I will give people a reassuring little talk about a healthy body's capacity to overcome infections, the impotence of antibiotics against viruses, and about the side effects of these drugs. Mostly, I'm ashamed to say, I inject antibiotics, and the client leaves happy to have been given something tangible for his money.

Paradoxically, under-dosing, in my opinion, is a more pervasive problem than over-prescribing. Give too much of a drug and you may cause nasty side effects, but give too little and it's useless. The most common cause of under-dosing is through the dispensing of ampicillin tablets and capsules (a cheap form of penicillin) – and, to a lesser extent, oxytetracycline, a cheap tetracycline – without informing the owner of the importance of dosing the drug on an empty stomach. These drugs are simply not absorbed if given with a lot of food, and I have seen cases where their failure to control infection could well have been due to such a mistake.

In general, the penicillins are very safe, and it's probably better to use a dose that errs on the high side than the reverse. Similarly, there are some conditions, such as bladder and skin infections, which might require long courses of antibiotics. The symptoms will possibly disappear after a few days of tablets, but will recur soon if treatment is prematurely discontinued. As a locum or junior veterinarian in a practice, dealing with another vet's cock-ups of this nature requires considerable tact, and after seeing the same mistake made again and again, it is all too easy for one's patience to run out, with dire consequences.[5]

---

[5] see Locums p98

Bandages

You've seen the animal charity advertisements? A cuddly, saccharinely cute puppy swathed in dazzlingly white bandages, gawping pathetically at the camera with big beseeching brown eyes. Have you ever wondered how the mutt was bandaged? Have you ever wondered how long the bandages stayed in that pristine state?

It was bandaged late one hot afternoon,[6] after the imbecile of an owner had let the pup (unvaccinated, naturally) gambol off the lead in a litter-strewn park. It defaecated (pooped) some worm eggs into the children's sandpit and then scratched sand over its glistening productions, cutting itself on the broken Buckfast bottle buried there by yobs. The wriggling bundle was then rushed to the surgery, jetting blood all over the waiting room floor, where the owner let it wander while waiting for a consultation.

The poor locum vet, already behind time, was told by the nurse to see the pup next. (Mrs. Z, a notoriously obnoxious harridan, and her equally repugnant Persian cat, had to wait a bit longer.) After wasting a few minutes trying to instruct the owner how to hold her delinquent charge, the vet called a nurse to help. She, torn from her coffee-and-fag break, was in a foul mood, something she did not attempt to disguise. Unceremo-

---

[6] see Weather p137

niously squashed to the table, the pup was finally still long enough for the vet to inspect and clean the small cut.

The vet's instinct was to use a staple gun to close the wound in an instant, but the nurse confirmed that the practice lacked such a modern gadget. As the pup had just been fed and the vet wanted to go home at some point that night anyway, a general anaesthetic and a stitch-up there and then was out of the question (the pup might vomit under anaesthetic and then choke to death). The only alternative: a bandage. The nurse sighed resentfully as the locum asked for this sort of wound dressing, and that sort of bandage roll, but eventually a suitable array of ingredients was assembled, and the bandaging proceeded, interrupted and reinitiated twice, because of the convulsions of the uncooperative mongrel. The owner was told to bring the pup back in three days, all going well, but immediately if the bandages became at all wet or soiled. (Theoretically this wasn't possible because clear instructions were issued to cover the affected leg with a thick plastic bag when the pooch needed out for a pee or a poo.)

A week later, the pup was returned to the surgery. The bandage was tattered, saturated and stinking, having been dashed in a puddle within moments of leaving the surgery. The leg was horribly infected. The receptionist did not book an extended appointment for bandage-changing (a client even less agreeable than Mrs. Z was waiting to be seen next). The leg was cleaned and re-bandaged, but the pup succumbed to Parvovirus[7] a week later anyway.

---

[7] see p117

Birds

They're often almost impossible to extract from their cages, extremely difficult to catch once out, and 'challenging' to examine properly. If you medicate the food or water they'll go hungry or thirsty rather than dose themselves. Injecting them is stressful both for them and for you. Parrots not only inflict awful injuries, but they shriek appallingly loudly, and they cost a fortune, so refer them to a specialist[8] if at all possible. Cockatiels die as soon as one looks at them. Psittacosis, carried by birds, kills people. Pigeon-fanciers can be demanding little know-it-alls. Best to give them what they want and show them the door.

During the summer months, members of the public constantly arrive with nestlings they have, in ignorance, stolen from their parents. If there are inexperienced nurses in the practice they may attempt to rear them, the ignorant little fools. Poorly feral pigeons (considered vermin by most municipalities) are dumped on veterinary practices the year round. If the nurses are squeamish you'll have to inject vitamin P,[9] otherwise do the sensible (and arguably more humane) thing and wring their necks.

Sometimes the strain of pointless bird consulta-tions is too much. Two young colleagues, of whom one

---

[8] see Specialists p125
[9] see Euthanasia p61

was on-call, were enjoying a game of snooker one evening when the inevitable happened – a call-out. Colleague A failed to persuade the anxious owner that her budgie could wait until the following day, and that the £80 call-out fee would be money ill-spent.

Colleague B insisted on accompanying Colleague A to the pensioner's flat, a malicious grin on his face – how dare someone destroy their evening off for something this trivial! The door was opened by a tremulous old woman, whose feathered sole companion was similarly infirm, listlessly perched in the bottom of a little cage, feathers fluffed. At least the diagnosis was clear: vague-sick-bird-syndrome.

Colleague A tried to look professional and competent as he reached in to grasp the ailing avian, although, of course, he had no more idea of how to approach this than the average vet – in other words, not a clue. Colleague B, meanwhile, had adopted the expression of a half-wit, with a cocked head and drooling mouth. When Colleague A was off-guard, struggling to maintain his thoughtful and concerned air as the budgie tweaked the skin at the edge of a fingernail (causing him extreme pain), Colleague B suddenly wrested the hapless 'Twinkie' from him, pulling a wing open and holding it up to the light.

'Doth it. . . f. . . f. . . fly?' he slurred, a gormless expression of wonder on his exaggeratedly-twisted face. Colleague A, mortified (not having downed the three pints that were lubricating his companion's bravura performance), pulled a rictus grin and, thinking quickly and blushing deeply, stammered,

'I'm really sorry, Mrs. Murdo, I have to look after him this evening. He's, he's. . . not quite right.' The

poor old lady's expression of horror transformed to one of sympathy.

Colleague A retrieved the bird, prescribed some vitamin drops and medicated seed, and tried to conclude business as quickly as possible, while Colleague B staggered around the old dear's flat, picking up ornaments, smelling, tapping and tasting them at random, throwing in a moan every now and again for good measure. . . To cut the story slightly short, the friendship took a long time to recover; I'm not sure whether the budgie was as resilient.

Bosses, and Running Your Own Business

Vets who choose to stay in practice may eventually own their own surgeries. They could set up as a one-vet affair, they might employ assistants, or they could go into partnership with another vet. In my experience partners often fall out. This is unsurprising, given the intensely personal nature of vetting and the idiosyncratic approaches that many people have. Add to this the economic pressures of running a business. . .

The worst melt-down I am aware of resulted in the junior partner taking a position with a rival practice but insisting that the original business change its phone numbers so that the clients would not automatically be retained by his former partner!

As a locum I have worked for many one-vet affairs. If a vet has been working solo for several years you can expect that he or she will be highly stressed due to the long hours and the financial and emotional pressures. The staff will regale you with tales of this vet's eccentric behaviour, and you may well be appalled by the extremely old-fashioned or negligent approach revealed by the case records.

The good thing about a sole-charge locum is that generally you have no one looking over your shoulder (assuming your employer is away recovering in a sanatorium or something). The worst-case scenario is when he or she 'just wants to take a bit of time off to fix things up around the practice'. The poor locum will constantly have the neurotic eye of an unstable obsessive looking over their shoulder. Sometimes these sole-practitioner businesses seek to take on another vet. Because they are very out of date and highly idiosyncratic they will only employ brand new graduates, who (with luck, they hope) will not know any better and whom they can corrupt without difficulty.

Eventually many solo operators break down completely. I once worked for the receivers who had taken over such a failed practice. The hapless vet in question had apparently started out as extremely enthusiastic and competent, notably good at surgery. He became a hopeless alcoholic. Obviously he lost many of his clients, but, towards the end, there were apparently still a loyal few: those who came in the morning because he was relatively sober early in the day, and those who came in the evening because the DTs had worn off as his blood-alcohol levels climbed. He prepared syringes containing an antibiotic-corticosteroid cocktail,[10] so his remaining staff told me, and everything that wasn't in for vaccination would receive this magical cure-all. When calling clients from the waiting room he would hiss at his receptionist to tell him who was there, so that he could pretend

---

[10] The traditional standby of some older vets.
The corticosteroid has harmful side effects but makes the patient feel better (see Steroids p127) and the antibiotic helps if there's a bacterial infection (there probably isn't but the more that's injected the more that can be charged).

to recognise them – his eyesight had long since gone. He took ages to thread needles as not only could he not see but he was invariably shaking. Mid-operation he would sometimes leave his unqualified staff tending anaesthetised animals and nip to the pub next door for a top-up.

So what manner of person stays in the veterinary profession long enough to own a share in – or, indeed an entire – practice? Unfortunately it all too often seems to be someone who has run out of all enthusiasm for the hands-on side of things, and is obsessed with profits, but has no concept of business management, or the management of personnel, but who appears utterly charming to his or her clients. As far as making money is concerned, a common practice is to re-sterilise syringes to the point where every second one leaks.

Some veterinary bosses seem to use fear and humiliation as their major management tools. For these demons, public haranguing is the standard method of correcting even the most trivial of errors. More than one veterinarian and nurse in more than one practice has told me of being reduced to tears by the boss in full tyrant mode.

As in all organised fields of human activity, there is a tendency to visit the horrors of the past on the new blood, using such hackneyed phrases as: 'You have it easy these days, when I. . . ' or 'It never did me any harm. . .'

The truth is, in 'his day' (I use 'his' because most older veterinarians are male) being on call was far easier. The clients were not nearly as demanding, not having viewed those horribly distorted and sanitised veterinary programmes on television, and there were probably fewer of them, so he could manage a week on the trot without becoming sleep-deficient.

I have to admit, even I have been guilty of inflicting some of the tortures of my early years on more junior veterinarians. When I was a student, we were sent in to the consulting rooms to examine a patient and make our diagnosis and then the vet would come in and point out all our mistakes, with the client present. I know I caused severe distress to at least one student 'seeing practice' by using this method, the miserable whingeing little wimp! Why, in my day. . .

The abuse of feminine loyalty appears to be pervasive. In my experience, women seem to feel a much deeper sense of loyalty to a practice than do men. This gives the unscrupulous employer free licence to extract unpaid overtime from them, and pay abysmally low wages. This applies particularly to nursing and reception staff.[11] This may not be the forum to venture further into the social and psychological reasons for feminine forbearance – or should one say complicity? – but I'd like to call on women to stand up for their rights. Unite, and don't let the bastards do you down!

Young school drop-outs who 'love animals' are

---

[11] Just before the introduction of the minimum wage, I knew of one boss who used to pay some of the female staff £1.80 an hour and would occasionally assault them if he imagined that they had misbehaved in any way, grabbing them by the backs of their necks and squashing their faces into the nearest table. None of them took any action against him as they were terrified of losing their jobs in that very poor area, did not want to abandon their colleagues, and were restricted by local family commitments.

ready victims for exploitation. In fact there are so many of them willing to work for virtually nothing that many practices run on these poor sub-nurse drudges. When they become disillusioned, or ask for more money (such naivety!) the boss turfs them out into the street and takes in another willing dupe.

They are not the only people to suffer from this system. It's stressful in the extreme for the assistant veterinarian to continually have to explain the most basic of animal care tasks to these willing-but-unable girls (as they invariably are). They are prone to cooing for what seems like hours over the fluffy kittens and puppies, rather than lifting the old paralysed dogs out of their ordure. What's worse, to accompany their lack of work they often insist on a background of moronically gabbling DJs, when all you want is peace and quiet, and above the racket they are perpetually discussing their diets. None of them eats breakfast, so come 11 am they're feeling faint, which is no damn good if you're needing a firm pair of hands on a Rottweiler.[12] Give me the boss who pays decent wages to decent qualified nursing staff any day!

Penny-pinching doesn't just apply to staffing costs. Resterilising disposable syringes is all very well, but when it comes to only one in two of the syringes on one's consulting room shelves being usable, it's highly embarrassing! There will also be pressure to use the same syringe to administer more than one drug at a time. In practices where this is the rule, have a look at the bottom of the bottles of Synulox (a broad-spectrum antibiotic). You will see a horrible brown deposit. This may be due to water from wet syringes

---

[12] see Dogs p46

reacting with the Synulox. The very expensive antibiotic is now useless, but do they know and do they care? Less effective treatment perhaps means a longer course, which means more money. . . but perhaps that's too devious, even for the average head of a practice! Cheap paper drapes (used to screen off a cleaned area for surgery) are an irritation in the extreme when they become blood-soaked and disintegrate, but some practices don't even use drapes, and use the same instruments for several operations.

Then the dogs will come back to the practice with 'reactions to the catgut'! Your boss will say things like 'This is very unusual, I've never seen anything like it before!' and he'll expect you to sing the same mendacious song. One money-hungry vet I knew (adored by his loyal clients because he always appeared cheerful and always made a fuss of their animals) insisted that every animal HAD to have an injection, regardless of what was wrong with it, and, furthermore, that every animal had a follow-up appointment. Needless to say, I didn't last long in that practice.

Cats

Cats not only bite, defaecate, urinate and discharge their anal glands as defence/attack mechanisms, but they also scratch. This makes the nervous cat a far more difficult and dangerous proposition than the nervous dog. Reaching into the cat box to withdraw such a fury is as appealing as thrusting one's arm into a food processor – correction, it's less attractive because food processors are generally hygienic. Cats' teeth and claws are veritable pathogen paradises, delayed-action germ warfare: today you may be happy that you've escaped with a few scratches, tomorrow you'll be unable to work with the pain and the swelling.

When shredding flesh gets boring, the furiously flailing felid will often enter Houdini mode, and bolt for the nearest hiding place (or, worse, away forever if you've been careless and left a door or window open). Extricating a frenzied escapee from the back of a cupboard full of bags of dog food, glassware and pill bottles, while attempting to present yourself as a dignified, competent and confident exponent of a noble profession is not easy. At moments like this I bite my lips and imagine myself lying on a beach in the sun somewhere. . . anywhere other than on my knees dripping blood in a chaotic veterinary surgery with a distraught client on the verge of tears breathing down my neck, dogs fighting in the waiting room outside, a visit booked in my longed-for lunch[13] break, a client to apologise to concerning the non-arrival of laboratory results, a severe headache. . . [14]

[13] see Lunch p101
[14] see A Typical Day p143

Cat Lovers

Cats are weakly social small carnivores. The attraction these wildlife destroyers hold for weakly social human beings is a fascinating phenomenon. In my experience, this attraction is inversely proportional to a person's capacity for abstract thought and to their emotional stability. My reasons for putting the cat among the pigeons in this way are derived from direct experience of cat freaks.

Let's start with the observation that cat lovers usually consider themselves to be 'animal lovers'. We need to determine first of all what is meant by the term 'animal lover'. Does it mean someone who cares about the quality of life of all animals, or someone who wants to preserve animal life at all costs? If it's either of these then the cat lover in question has clearly not realised that cats are obligate carnivores, and has not seen the horrors inflicted on those creatures whose processed remains find their way into cat food.

There is brutality at many stages of the meat production process. I've seen cattle being dehorned, I've seen them being loaded onto trucks with cattle prods, I've seen the terror-stricken creatures being forced towards the final crush at the abattoir, I've seen the poorly stunned (*i.e.* still conscious) animals thrashing upside down in agony, suspended by a hind leg, as the blood spurts from a severed carotid artery (ruminants have a vertebral artery which can keep the brain supplied with oxygen for seconds after the carotid is cut). How many cat lovers (or meat eaters, for that matter) even think about, far less see, where meat comes from?

OK, the conclusion from this little rant is that if cat lovers are 'animal lovers', then 'animal lover' cannot pertain to those who are concerned about preserving the length or quality of animal life in general. The only other meaning for the phrase that I can come up with is someone who is attracted to and cares about only the creatures immediately around him or her, and this means turning a blind eye to the mutilated mice, butchered blackbirds and ripped-open rabbits. But, for me, the darkest side of this 'animal-loving' is that it can accompany a disregard for, or ignorance of, one's fellow man. Much of mankind lives in protein-deficient poverty, and here, in the obscenely wealthy 'developed' world, subsidised by debt repayments from the 'developing' world (those debts deliberately induced by the developed world), [15] we are stuffing high quality protein (from grain-fed animals) down the throats of horribly corpulent cats and terminally tubby terriers.[16]

---

[15] see 'Confessions of an Economic Hitman' by John Perkins, Ebury Press 2006
[16] see Obesity p105

You might argue that most of the above could apply equally to dog owners. Not necessarily: it is possible for dogs to live healthily on an entirely vegetarian diet. I did once hear of an idiot who insisted on feeding his cat such a diet. According to the vet who told me the story (without revealing the identity of the person, I hasten to add) this ignoramus refused all advice and his cat wasted away and died. . . And he probably thought of himself as a cat-lover!

To continue with the anecdotal evidence, the one-sided bonding phenomenon that lonely unstable people have with their cats is sometimes extended to include the veterinarian who looks after the objects of worship. This syndrome might be triggered on a particularly good day, when you're just about to leave for a trip to Paris, for example, and it's been unusually quiet. Thus, oozing *bonhomie* and *joie de vivre*, you succeed in charming the old lady who brings in her very thin, very old cat. Said animal, for reasons known only to itself, decides not to transform into a scratching spitting fury today when retrieved from the depths of its noisome basket. The old dear says, 'Oh, he must really like you! He didn't like the last vet, you know, he was very rough.'

You say nothing, but already, the warning bells are tinkling. The klaxons go off when, returning depressed from your holiday, you see your initials on the case record laid out in anticipation of the appointment. The client has requested YOU, and no one but you, to look at poor little Suki. The problem is that all creatures are mortal, and poor little Suki, suffering from terminal kidney failure, is a barely respiring manifestation of the evanescence of this worldly existence. You are now on a pedestal. You are a god who can confer immortality. The plaintive '. . . but you'll do your best for him?' issuing from the withered lips, tells you that your attempts to convey the news of probable imminent demise are to no avail.

The most you can hope for is that the creature dies peacefully at home, and that there will be no repercussions. The worst possible outcome is for the quality of life of the failing felid to deteriorate to the extent that even the owner recognises this, and requests that you put the creature down, and then for the euthanasia process to go wrong. . . Either it's a home visit and you find yourself on hands and knees trying to grab a terrified skeleton scrabbling to the furthest reaches of the urine-soaked carpet under the cat hair-festooned communal bed (owner and seventeen cats), or the diarrhoeic pissing pussy throws a fit on the consulting room table and won't let itself be restrained for the fatal needle. At this point the owner also throws a tantrum, screaming, 'You're killing him, you're killing him!'

'What did you think I was doing, silly old cow? And your effing screaming doesn't help calm him down!' This is what you want to say, but you and the nurse exchange looks, and battle on professionally. In the waiting room outside, the yowls and screams have a large audience. . . 'God, why do I do this job?' you think to yourself? Good question.

Another perversity of some 'cat lovers' is that they refuse to have their noxious vermin neutered, believing it cruel. The operation is performed under a general anaesthetic, it lasts a few minutes, and the cat is right as rain within a day or two. Compare that to the lives of hell suffered by groin-driven grimalkins, and testosterone turbo-charged toms. Fights and kittens galore: an appalling racket at night, abscesses, multiple infections (including 'Cat AIDS': FIV and FeLV, FIP *etc.*), premature senility, short lives. And what about the unwanted kittens, abandoned or drowned? Some owners will claim that they keep their unneutered tomcats inside all the time. If this is the case then these owners must have a very poor sense of smell!

Happily the cat charities approve of neutering, and some will capture feral cats and bring them in for de-sexing and release. I wholeheartedly approve of this. While, in an ideal world, it would be better to have no feral cats at all, in practice it is impossible to eliminate them, and the best option is to have a stable community of neutered territory holders.

Unfortunately the cat charity fanatics cannot be described as a stable community of territory holders themselves. I've never met a sphere of human activity so riven by petty rivalries and jealousies. I once made the *faux pas* of mistaking crazed representatives from Local Cat Fanatic Group A for loonies from Local Cat Fanatic Group B, these groups being the irreconcilable products of a bitter personality-propelled fission. That was not a mistake I ever repeated.

When one speaks to these people one has to consider all one's words and actions very, very carefully. They will analyse every nuance, and then say that the last vet told them something entirely different. One will then have to spend half an hour diplomatically picking one's way across a minefield of potential misunderstandings. Oh, the exhaustion and relief when they eventually leave the surgery! If children in the developing world received a tenth of the time, money and attention expended on terminally-ill feral carnivora by the good burghers of Britain, the leading cause of infant mortality would be sleep deprivation.

Charity Work[17]

These noble bodies exist to help animals belonging to the poor. The RSPCA, additionally, concerns itself with the welfare interests of animals in general. The PDSA requests a donation for the treatment of a client's beasts whereas the RSPCA charges a token fixed fee.

Working for one of these organisations, having worked in the average private veterinary practice, is akin to going over the top into enemy fire, after languishing in an uncomfortable but relatively safe trench. The doors open in the morning and a tsunami of Rottweilers, Pitbull Terriers, Parvovirus[18] and pandemonium crashes in. If an appointment system operates, this will be a ludicrous token affair. Each client will be assigned a hypothetical five or seven-and-half minute slot. Even if the receptionist manages to establish how many animals each client is bringing, and increases the time allocation accordingly, there is no way you'll stick to the schedule, as people won't hear when they're called (the waiting room will resemble an Hieronymus Bosch painting) and the inevitable tonnage of 'emergencies' will take precedence. As a consequence, towards the end of a session

---

[17] Essentially: working for the PDSA (People's Dispensary for Sick Animals) the RSPCA (Royal Society for the Prevention of Cruelty to Animals) and the SSPCA (Scottish Society for the Prevention of Cruelty to Animals)
[18] see p117

of consultations the average client will be furious, having been kept waiting for hours after the due time. Your first minute or two of the consultation will then be spent pacifying the owner. His Rottweiler will, of course, be beyond pacifying. . .

Communication with charity clients is often difficult. While the right-wing press delights in blaming people for falling by the wayside of our materialistic society, many recipients of charity have been dealt a poor hand in life, are poorly educated, and come equipped with assorted physical and mental problems. To make matters worse they will often smell worse than their animals. They will not have the attention span to follow an explanation of any length or complexity. You will be reduced to the level of saying: 'Your dog has fleas. Fleas! You see them? Here – look. There are hundreds of little dark things moving. These are fleas! Yes I know he's chewing himself. It's because he has fleas! Look! So, I'm giving you this spray, just follow the instr. . . No, just spray him once a week. . . Oh, no, I'll spray him now. Bring him back next week, OK? Bring him back in one week. Yes, I know his skin's sore. That's because he has fleas! I've just treated him. . . I've just killed the fleas with this spray. I'll give him an injection also to make him feel better. Alright? Yes, I know they're still moving, but when you get home. . . '

Some charity clients are barely capable of looking after themselves and yet they acquire huge and hungry dogs (a response, undoubtedly, to low self-esteem), and your job is to patch these unruly creatures up, and send them back 'home' again, to wander the streets, fighting, contracting diseases, attacking children and causing car accidents.

The PDSA believes that anyone taking on an animal should be willing to pay a private vet for vaccination[19] and neutering[20], and therefore until recently, when a pilot scheme was introduced, the PDSA did not vaccinate or neuter animals other than tomcats. This was all very well, but people don't have their animals vaccinated or neutered. In the malnourished Omega-3-deprived and chronic-poverty-damaged mind of the average Rottweiler owner, there's a much bigger chance of him winning a fortune with a scratchcard (then all his problems would be over. . .) than of his dog succumbing to a fatal infection. Wrong. The lottery is an evil institution and all those behind it should be par-boiled and fed to Rottweilers!

Of course, not all those who use the services of the PDSA or the RSPCA are poor. Survey the cars parked outside the barricaded fortress of the veterinary centre and you'll see the odd flashy late-reg. Mercedes, Jaguar *etc*. Most likely one of the nurses or receptionists will know the reason for this affluence, but be unable to prove it: X is a big-time drug dealer;[21] Y is an expert at cheating on benefits. . . The only practical way to deal with people like this is to publicly shame them. I've seen a feisty little nurse pull this off successfully with a particularly pecunious pusher. In the waiting room, as she handed his repaired 'grotty' back to him, she remarked casually to the receptionist how it was amazing that some people had the gall to turn up at

---

[19] see Vaccinations p133
[20] see Spaying p124
[21] This is all too common in these poor areas where the only escape from the depressing environment is often the temporary and illusory one offered by gambling, drugs and alcohol, something with which some vets can empathise!

the surgery in a really expensive car, and then only make a measly 50p donation. He handed over a £20 note and left in a hurry.

In summary, in these situations the vet only has time for the most basic of healthcare, and most of this is dealing with things that could be prevented by neutering, vaccination or common sense. There is a sensation of sprinting flat-out just to stay in the same spot, as one drips yet another puking purging Parvo pup, or tries to alert another halitotic alcoholic to the virtues of basic dental care as you yank a canine from his similarly acrid cur's cankerous chops[22]. Even if one had the time for more intellectually stimulating diagnostic and therapeutic protocols, the means would be lacking. Charities run on strict budgets, and by the end of the week you'll probably be out of even basic antibiotics. Without extensive reform of our pluto-cratic society, where those at the bottom of the tree are set against each other by our neo-liberal capitalist popular press, there's little hope of making any real progress.

[22] see Teeth p129

Corpses

Why does no veterinary practice ever seem to have an efficient corpse-disposal system? The average small animal veterinarian possibly generates a hundred kilos of carcase a day, most of this material coming from the consulting rooms.

After euthanasia[23] and client-comforting, you have to bag the body. This is easy enough in the case of mice, rabbits and guinea pigs but Mastiffs, Rottweilers and Great Danes are a different proposition. They're impossible to bag on your own, and difficult enough for two, if you are fortunate enough to have someone to help (rare in the average practice, where several people are nursing sore backs). You can try sliding the leviathan, front first, off the table, while coaxing the bag over the forelegs and head. If you succeed here, all your luck for the day will now be exhausted, and the bag will burst. The boss will recently have decided to 'save money' by using cheaper bags. Now you'll need to use four bags instead of one! And then, perhaps some extra over the hindquarters. When you eventually get to the point of dragging the body away, the bags will come off, or tear again, spilling urine and faeces, which you will tread in.

The storage area for the corpses is usually in a back room somewhere, along what feels like several miles of

---

[23] see p61

corridors and through umpteen doors. At least one of the side doors will be ajar, and clients will be able to see through the doorway as beloved Benji bumps backwards and upside down along the floor, half covered by a shredded garbage bag, leaving a slick of mixed excrement and saliva. (Of course you can forget about trolleys. They cost money!) Exhausted, you arrive at the freezer. This will be a conventional deepfreeze, necessitating that you lift the 80 kilo-gramme burden (13 stones) a metre in order to tip it over the edge to rest on top of several previously processed rigid frigid Rottweilers. By this point your back is screaming, but somehow you lever the tonnage over the rim.

It is only now that you notice that one of the bags already in the freezer is labelled 'Leave accessible: PM to be performed. . . ' and today's date is written there. A titanic bout of sumo wrestling sees the labelled carcass out to thaw, and you stagger back to the consulting room, over the disgustingly streaked floor, to put down another monster.

OK, a few practices have walk-in cold storage rooms, but then these are usually stuffed to the ceiling with precarious mountains of bursting carcase bags. I'd rather go skiing at Klosters *danke*, at least some of that is fun!

Dogs

The diversity of dog breeds mirrors the multiplicity of
human interests and aspirations. While these may be
worthy (Labrador Retrievers used as Guide Dogs for
the Blind, for example), they are frequently ignoble
(*e.g.* Pit-Bull Terriers). Additionally, every deviation
from the body plan and psychology of the ancestral
wolf seems to bring its set of own problems. If you
look at one of those dog-breed guide books lying
around a veterinary waiting room, you'll see only the
positive features of every breed listed. Euphemisms
will gloss over the appalling flaws that mar some of
these perverted wolves. Here's a key to interpreting
some of the more blatant whitewashing:

What the chart says	What it means
Affectionate	Utterly stupid and untrainable
Good with children	As above
Intensely loyal	Paranoid xenophobe, attacks all strangers (of whatever species) on sight
Needs a lot of exercise	Will destroy your house and garden
Lively	Hysterical
Lap dog	Stupid, frail, with bulging eyes, appalling teeth and knees, and a hideously irritating yap
Beautiful long coat	You will have to spend half your waking hours brushing the damn thing and the other half vacuuming your carpets

Let's look at a few of the more common breeds as the veterinarian sees them.

Border Collies
These are genuinely intelligent animals which need a lot of mental stimulation as well as exercise. Often the (non-shepherd) owner is a sedentary moron, and as a result the dog is dominant, aggressive and unmanageable. I've put down many physically healthy border collies because their poor socialisation and lack of training at the hands of idiots has rendered them dangerously unmanageable.

Bulldogs
These suffer from horrendous breathing problems and intractable skin infections buried amongst all the wrinkles. Midnight caesareans will result in more puppies, which will grow up to require midnight caesareans themselves. . . The breed should be banned, but people love them because the squashed faces appeal to their mothering instincts and the pups sell for hundreds of pounds each. I once worked alongside a vet who had, quite against his inclinations, earned himself the reputation of 'Bulldog expert'. The poor man was driven to distraction by the respiratory, cardiac, dermatological and reproductive problems of this monstrously cruel breed, and by the twisted and often mercenary people associated with it.

Chihuahuas and Toy Pomeranians
Terrifyingly vicious little brutes sometimes, and bloody difficult to muzzle. Should be banned.

German Shepherds
Puppy farmers churn out hundreds of these poor creatures with appalling hip problems. This is often exacerbated by the deterioration of the spinal cord as

they age (CDRM or chronic degenerative radiculo-myelopathy, which might be related to multiple sclerosis in humans). Progressive hindquarter paralysis and incontinence follow. If the owner has any sense the dog will be put out of its misery, rather than left to eke out its existence lying helplessly in a pool of excrement.

Greyhounds
Racing greyhounds tend to be fed very mushy food, and end up with disgusting teeth. In their racing days these dogs may well be viewed as economic units, nothing more and nothing less, so if you can't guarantee complete recovery you'll need to take out the vitamin P.[24] If you're unfortunate enough to have to work at a greyhound track, expect to meet some uncouth and unscrupulous characters who will not be particularly courteous if you pull their dogs from a race. The dogs themselves tend to be friendly, but they scream as soon as you lay a hand on them – the reaction to an ordinary subcutaneous injection is deafening.

Labrador Retrievers
This breed is generally friendly, but the most vicious dog I ever came across was a Labrador. For some reason Labrador owners like stuffing their pets to barrage balloon proportions, and the dogs suffer accordingly.[25]

Rottweilers
'Grotties', I call them: macho accessories of the inadequate – never trust these dogs or their owners. The owner will tell you: 'He's friendly, don't worry!'

---

[24] see Euthanasia p61
[25] see Obesity p105

Bullshit. Get him to go away and come back another day with the monster muzzled. With any luck you'll never see the dog again, because the client will find it impossible to fit a muzzle. If he does return, leave the case card for another vet, and deal with the Cavalier King Charles Spaniel and its anal glands instead. Never believe an owner who claims to be able to restrain his dog for you. Unless he is a titanic muscle-bound hulk himself, it's impossible for one person to restrain a healthy adult grotty. On the good side, in my experience grotties generally growl before they attack. Heaven help you when they do attack! Rottweilers should be banned.

OK, alright, I have met several well-trained Rottweilers owned by decent, intelligent people, but

49

I'd rather you were careful than have your mutilation on my conscience!

Samoyeds

Generally owned by fools who keep them indoors in centrally heated houses and then wonder why they pant a lot. If this breed had any more hair you'd have difficulty finding the animals inside all the packaging. Having said that, you'd locate the beasts easily even in snowdrifts (where these poor 'sheep-dogs' would feel more comfortable) by virtue of their piercing barks. I once had the terrible misfortune to give a Samoyed pup its first vaccination in a small and bare consulting room. The high-pitched 'yip' it repeatedly emitted was amplified and echoed by the bare walls of what, for me, became a veritable torture chamber. I jump at the least noise, and certainly I could not control my involuntary blink-and-wince every time the brainless fluff-ball vocalised, no matter how hard I tried to keep my happy puppy-greeting face in place (No.6 in the repertoire). The owner complained that I 'clearly hated her dog' and my boss called me in to explain myself. Well, the upshot is that now I hate the entire goddamn breed! Good thing, though – with global warming I think these horribly hirsute hounds will become extinct.

Spaniels

All spaniels are always suffering from anal gland problems and many from lipfold pyoderma (nasty smelly infection of the lower lip). Cocker Spaniels have mercurial temperaments, and will be friendly one moment and exploring the internal anatomy of your hand with their dental apparatus the next. Springers are either very friendly or the opposite. Both Cockers and Springers suffer from execrable ear problems. The reek will take days to disappear, both from your hands and from the consulting room.

Cavalier King Charles Spaniels, apart from having the worst anal glands[26] of any breed, have the worst hearts. Their valves are as effective at stopping blood flowing the wrong way as veterinary training is at equipping one to handle the stresses of the job.

Yorkshire Terriers

The worst mouths and knees of any breed are possessed by these straggle-haired child-substitutes. The foulness of their foetid festering gums and calculus-caked teeth has to be seen and smelt to be believed, and yet, incredibly, owners will frequently kiss the putrid maws of their grossly neglected, but superficially adored, carious little angels.

In the process of stunting the breed sufficiently to appeal to perverted parenting instincts, the legs have been distorted, such that the kneecaps often rub along unmerrily on the insides of the cruelly twisted limbs. Add obesity and you have severe arthritis (strictly 'arthrosis'): hey presto, hop-along halitosis is the instant diagnosis!

Artmeier's non-linear proportionality rule of dog magnitude and owner intellectual capacity

For dogs smaller than a Jack Russell Terrier, size is directly proportional to the owner's intelligence, whereas for dogs bigger than a Labrador, size is inversely related to the owner's intelligence.

---

[26] see p18

Drips
(Intravenous Fluid Therapy)

In theory the best way to treat shock, dehydration *etc.*
is to set up an intravenous drip. They work fairly well
if your patient requires a very high rate of infusion
and is comatose. Unfortunately both these conditions
are seldom met. Drips certainly do not work in
gyrating puppies, which is when you're most likely to
want to use them.

As a veterinary student one is taught how to assess
the hydration status of animals and calculate appropriate drip rates. Forget all this. Unless you are lucky
enough to have an electronic drip machine and a
stationary patient it's useless knowledge. A slowish
drip will stop within an hour, even if the animal hasn't
pulled it out or tied the drip lead in knots. You can
spend fifteen minutes trying to set the drip at five
drops a minute, or whatever ludicrously slow rate
you've calculated, only for the animal to shift its
position slightly and the drip to stop altogether or
shoot up to 120 drops a minute. Every new graduate
goes through anguish until she realises that the best
she can do is to give her charge a large amount of fluid
in the first half an hour, and then let it sink or swim
thereafter. . . Well, that's not entirely true. There is
always the intraperitoneal route. One jabs a needle (or
catheter) into the abdomen and fills it drum-tight with

fluids. Bingo, the newly paunched pup needs no more fluids for the next 24 hours, no matter how much gunk emerges from each end! You can even send it home! The problem is finding nurses[27] willing to hold the animal while you inject all this fluid.

---

[27] see p103

Drug Abuse

There are compensations to being a vet. When things get really bleak, one can always find something interesting to inject or swallow. If you've resorted to alcohol in the evening (OK, during the day also!), try some dog arthritis tablets the next morning – they do wonders for the hangover. If you're throwing up, give yourself a shot of dog anti-vomiting stuff. If you just generally feel awful there are always the morphine derivatives. Most practices have a good selection.

Are too many drugs giving you an irregular heart-beat? There'll be some tablets to sort that out also. Of course you'll need to wear a long-sleeved operating gown to cover up the needle tracks, and there are only so many times you can spin that tale about accidentally smashing the vials of Vetergesic at the greyhound stadium. . . Still, there's always vitamin P as a last resort. . . [28]

Sadly, this outlook is all too often the reality. Stress can climb to an intolerable level.[29]

---

[28] see Euthanasia p61
[29] Helpline numbers are given in the Introduction p8

Ears

Few owners seem to have the sense to keep an eye on their pets' ears. Few vets seem to show the owners how to clean their pets' ears or how to apply ear drops properly. It's always me that has to pick up the pieces, after months of neglect or ineffective treatment. Why, why, why!? I'm sick of it!

'OK, you need to hold the ear flap up like this. No, like this. Right, now put a good squirt of ear cleaner in. No, I don't care what the other vet told you, three drops is not enough! A good squirt. Now comes the most important part: you have to rub the ear from the bottom up-wards. Can you hear it squelching? No, not like that. You should be able to feel the ear funnel between your thumb and forefinger, right? Now the idea is that you milk all the muck up towards the top. Never put pressure on when you go down the way because you can damage the eardrum. No, not quite, let me show you again. . . Right, now take a wad of cottonwool, not a cottonbud, and reach in with your finger. As long as it's just your finger you can reach in as far as you can go. Now wipe it out. That's it! Do you see all the dirt? Now we'll do it a few more times, and then we can put the drops in. . . OK, now we rub again after we've put the drops in, and I'm sure if you continue doing it like this the ear will be fine in a week or two. . . '

Repeat that scene five to ten times a day, six days a week on average, and tell me you wouldn't get fed up. It's almost a relief when the dog is in such agony that one can't go anywhere near the ears. So it's the good old steroids and antibiotics[30] and re-examine next week. . .

If it's a kitten coming in for its first vaccination, it's probably got earmites. Sometimes there is so much wax in reaction to these parasites that it'll take you twenty minutes just to do the ears. Imagine your anger if it's in that state when it comes in for its second vaccination – another vet must have seen this animal previously but never checked the ears, the incompetent lazy bastard! (Then you see the signature on the card and realise it was you. . . Oops!)

Now you're earning the reputation of being extremely slow: 'Twenty-five minutes and it was only a vaccination! Tut, tut, Josh. The other vet does those in six.' Not a good start in a new practice, and, no, they won't understand if you try to explain it to them.

Aural haematomas (othaematomas, or blood blisters on the ears) are very common, particularly in dogs, and are often triggered by vigorous head-shaking, possibly secondary to ear infections or ear mite infestations, but not necessarily. There are a variety of surgical techniques, including the placement of multiple mattress sutures, the use of buttons or pieces of x-ray film on each side of the earflap to hold the ear flat, and the punching of a small hole and the insertion of a drain. They all work to some extent

---

[30] see pp127, 21

but if you're lucky enough not to be forced to adopt the practice's method, then opt for the hole-punch and drain insertion, because the others take bloody ages, and I mean 'bloody' ages!

The other common sort of ear operation is called 'ablation of the vertical section of the external ear canal'. This involves opening up the first part of the ear canal to the outside, and may be required when years of neglected inflammation have caused the lining of the canal to thicken to the extent that the ear is completely blocked. There isn't so much blood during this operation, but it's quite finicky work placing all the stitches.

However well the operations go, it can be hellish re-examining ears a few days later. If the owner has followed instructions and left the bucket collar in place things might still be holding together, but the owner won't have managed to get anywhere near the ear to clean it, and you'll find it hard enough yourself. The ear and the inside of the bucket collar will be encrusted with a mixture of wax and clotted blood, and it'll take ages for you to remove all this muck. Get someone else[31] to do it if you can!

---

[31] see Nurses p103

Ethics and Motivation

Why do people become vets? Some undoubtedly relish the challenge of diagnosing and treating difficult cases, some perhaps care about the wellbeing of animals, others want to help people by looking after their animals. Unfortunately none of these aspirations is likely to be satisfactorily fulfilled by being a practising veterinarian.

Potential vets are selected on the basis of their academic ability. On average, this means that vets are reasonably intelligent, and require intellectual stimulus to maintain an acceptable emotional state. Most veterinary tasks, as ought to be apparent from this book, are horribly mundane. After the first year or two of mastering the art of evacuating anal glands *etc.*, there is little in the way of such stimulation. Those cases that require great efforts at diagnosis and treatment will be too expensive for the owner to want to pursue, or your practice will lack the equipment to perform the appropriate investigations or treatments.

Assuming that neither of these checks exist, there remains the question of the morality of expending a great deal of time and money on an animal whose natural lifespan is much shorter than a human being's anyway, and which is likely to be suffering during the probably extended diagnosis and treatment, in a world where many people are deprived of basic healthcare. I would go so far as to say that pursuit of intellectual satisfaction for its own ends would be defined as immoral by most systems of ethics.

Let's assume that one's driving force is to reduce the sum of animal suffering in this world. In that case one would discourage people from keeping carnivores, or at the very least, encourage those who keep carnivores to feed them only flesh from animals which have been humanely reared and slaughtered. If one takes this argument to its logical extreme then one would discourage the keeping of any pets – the more animals in existence the more potential suffering. This is hardly likely to endear one to a potential employer or to potential clients.

There will, of course, be some cases where one can significantly alleviate animal suffering, whether by treatment, euthanasia, or owner education, but I can assure the aspirant veterinarian that these will be more than balanced by those cases where the owner refuses treatment or, against one's advice, insists on unduly prolonging a painful existence. It is very difficult indeed to modify the behaviour or change the entrenched beliefs of adult human beings. Remember also, that the average member of the public has an IQ of 100, which means that many of your clients will have IQs significantly below that. Communication on any level, far less the transmission of basic concepts of animal care, is frustrating to say the least. Thus, you, the small animal veterinarian, will inevitably be an accomplice in cruelty, willing or otherwise. Your employer will expect you to earn your salary, not to put every second patient immediately out of its owner-inflicted misery. Besides, the fewer prolonged complicated cases, the more boring your job will be. . . Read the previous paragraph!

In fact, I sincerely believe that even if your sole concern is the welfare of animals (let's face it, they're easy to love as they cannot be blamed for the world's problems), then in order to be effective in the long term, you must focus on people. Disenfranchised, badly educated and starving people are not likely to be overly concerned about animals. Few significant animal welfare issues require specialist veterinary knowledge to resolve – they need compassion, common sense and the economic wherewithal to take action.

This leads nicely to the next point. If your motive in becoming a vet is primarily to help people, then why do it in such an indirect and inefficient manner? The perversity of the (mis)appropriation of resources for the welfare of domestic animals in a world where many people are deprived of clean water, sanitation, food and basic medical care has already been pointed out. Guide Dogs for the Blind, Hearing Dogs for the Deaf, horses owned by Riding for the Disabled and similar worthy creatures are never going to be more than a small proportion of any practice's patients.

So, if you want to help people – and, I would argue, help animals more effectively in the long run – then campaign to have the developing world's debts annulled, become a doctor and work for *Medecins sans Frontières*, become a teacher, join Amnesty International, campaign for the narrowing of the gap between the rich and poor, or even work as a vet for Overseas Development Aid improving the efficiency of pastoralism in arid countries. . . but don't practise as a vet in the UK.

Euthanasia

Killing animals is a very large part of a veterinarian's life. Initially the thought of killing something may seem repugnant to the callow aspirant veterinarian. Don't worry, after your first ten PTSs (put-to-sleeps, or, as I say, 'poorly? – tough sh*ts'), it'll be just another ordinarily highly stressful part of your job.

In fact it often comes as a relief when a client concurs with a diagnosis of Vitamin P deficiency (*i.e.* gives permission for the administration of an overdose of pentobarbitone) rather than insisting on the continued treatment of the fitting 18-year-old skeletal Sheba with non-functioning kidneys. You know for certain that you are, at last, relieving suffering!

The standard spiel goes something like this:

'Now, we'll just give Mitzi an overdose of anaesthetic into the leg vein. I'll just clip the hair off here so that it's easier to find. Oops! Perhaps we'd better get a muzzle. I'll just get a nurse to help here... there we go. Now I'll just get the nurse to raise the vein for me. If he'd... oh, I'm sorry, I mean if she'd just hold still a moment... No it doesn't really hurt. She just doesn't like being held.'

At this point you start sweating.

'There we go. Now his... her... um, the heart

will stop almost immediately, but she may take a few deep breaths and there might be some muscle trembling.'

The dog gasps horribly, trembles, defaecates and urinates, and the owner is extremely distressed.

'Don't worry, mmm. . . lost consciousness immediately, these are just reflexes. The thing to keep at the top of your mind is that mmm's now completely out of suffering. You must have looked after. . . Mitzi did very well to get to this age.'

At this point you are definitely lying – the owner has left the poor creature in agony for weeks, at least.

For ten minutes or more, the owner will sob in your consulting room, telling you about all the beloved pet's endearing foibles. This will be the fifth time that day that you've been through this, the 26th time that week, the 92nd time that month. . . yet you'll have to look interested and caring, and not show any impatience even if there are thirty irate and impatient clients, with their multiple fighting pe(s)ts, in the waiting room outside. When you eventually get rid of the distraught ex-dog owner, you have the problem of the corpse. Then, a week later, you might receive a thank-you card and a box of chocolates. That's when a 'bumping' goes well. By now you, the reader, should be well enough schooled in the things which could go wrong to be able to imagine them unaided. . .

Exotics

There's an excited twittering amongst the reception staff today, a whispering behind raised hands. A self-conscious, gawky teenage boy sits in the corner of the waiting room with a big wooden box on his lap. The card is marked for you, because he's brought a python, and none of the other vets feels comfortable handling snakes. Already you have a reasonable idea what the story will be.

Like yourself as a kid, the young fellow is a wildlife fanatic. He's read all the wildlife books in his local library. Ask him about the birds of New Guinea, the fossorial mammals of the North American plains, or the Scarabidae of Africa, and he'll be able to tell you something. For him, though, snakes have always had a special allure. After years of persuasion on his part, his parents have allowed him to buy a python. He's worked all his holidays to save the money, he's made the cage himself, and fitted it with a heater and thermostat. Then he went to the local petshop and exchanged hundreds of pounds for a Royal Python. Mistake!!!

The timid creature is coiled apathetically in the corner of its little prison. The skin is blistered and weeping. The breath rattles, and bubbles of mucus can be seen issuing from its glottis (the extension to its windpipe, which you can see when you open the mouth). It hasn't eaten or drunk since he purchased it three weeks ago. It was ill then. It's nearly dead now. You explain to him that these beautiful and passive beasts are caught, none too gently, in the wild, thousands of miles away. Their only defence against man is to coil up, hence their alternative name of 'ball python'. They are smuggled in to the country crammed into small containers. Those that survive the journey are in the minority. They are passed from crooked dealer to bent trader to shady petshop owner.

The latter knows nothing about snakes except their profit margin. He'll tell the gullible what they want to hear: 'She'll take dead mice very well. She was bred in captivity, and is used to being handled. She's in beautiful condition.' The gullible hand over their money, and the petshop owner is happy to restock.

You explain this to the chastened client. You give him the option of immediate euthanasia or prolonged and expensive treatment, which is unlikely to be successful (fluid therapy, the culture of the numerous bacteria likely to be present, the procurement of a very expensive antibiotic on the basis of the culture results, the treatment for worms and skin mites, the daily washing with a disinfectant. . .). Having seen so many die before, the conviction in your voice is telling, and he opts for the needle of mercy.

The receptionists are all bright-eyed and gigglygirly as you emerge from the consultation room bearing the sad little bag. They request a look. Unsmiling, you show them the pathetic body. Inside, you are weeping at the horrors of this world and your helplessness. You will have a drink or two this evening.

Fleas

Never in the field of bestial conflict have so many suffered so much because of something so small and so easily prevented.

It's amazing how much a visit to the pub enhances people's sensitivity to the status of their pets' health. Problems that have been tolerated, or have gone unnoticed for months, take on fearsome dimensions after a tipple in the Rat and Carrot. It's 11.30 pm. You've nearly finished your weekend on call for the PDSA. You were so exhausted that you decided, at 11pm, to risk washing off the day's accretion of miscellaneous excrement and going to bed, despite the frequency of late night calls. You've just fallen asleep.

BEEP, BEEP, BEEP!!! Your heart rate doubles and you fumble for the light switch and the pager. The message reads: 'Mrs. X, blah, blah. . . dog in distress, restless, whining. . . ' You stagger through to the telephone. Somehow you manage to decipher the incoherent voice and read between the lines. The whole story in a nutshell is:

dog + fleas + neglect

⇨ dog – hair – surface layer of skin + infection + pain + smell

⇨ (eventually) owner, lurching in from pub, is unable to ignore smell and distress of dog

⇨ panic-and-guilt-driven after-hours phone call pressurising vet to see dog IMMEDIATELY ('I think he's dying!' – note that charity clients do not have to pay after-hours surcharge!)

⇨ furious fatigued vet wracks brains to think what suitable pain-relieving medicaments might be in client's medicine cupboard:
1% hydrocortisone ointment? No.
Antihistamine tablets or ointment? No.
Calamine lotion? Yes! Bingo!

⇨ relieved vet manages to postpone seeing dog until next day, advising liberal application of said lotion and telling client lotion will take an hour or two to work (vet knows that effect will be equivocal, but by then client will be in drunken slumber, and vet will be in exhausted sleep!)

Three days later, the client appears at the surgery with the dog, and says aggressively, 'The treatment didn't work!'

Vet: What treatment?

Client: The camoline! [sic]

Vet: But I told you to bring him in on Monday so we could treat him properly! The calamine lotion was only to give him temporary relief!

Client: I couldn't get transport.

Vet: Well, anyhow, he's here now. Right. You see here that the underlying problem is fleas? He's damaged his skin because he's been chewing so much and now he's infected. This is what we call a 'hotspot'. We need to give him something to stop him itching and to treat the fleas.

Client: I treated him for fleas – I got a spray from the petshop.

Vet: Well, I'm afraid that it hasn't worked. We'll need to use something stronger. Can you remember what it was you used, and when you last treated him? [32]

Client: ★ ★ ★

Vet: Well, we'll assume you treated him a long time ago so it's safe to use something else. Now, in order to get rid of fleas we need to kill both the fleas on your dog, and the part of the life cycle on the bedding and the carpets. The eggs and the baby fleas live there, and if we just kill the adults on the dog, then they'll be back again soon. You'll need to get a spray for him,

---

[32] Of course, the client hasn't a clue. In any case, in my experience, none of the flea treatments available in pet shops ever works. This could be because people don't follow the instructions, or perhaps they are all fundamentally useless. I don't know, but I'm utterly sick of that never-ending refrain: '. . . But I used a spray/shampoo/powder from the pet shop!' Someone must die for this, whether it's the companies that make inert products, the petshop owners who flog worthless trash with no conscience, or the incompetent morons who fail to follow basic instructions!

and a spray for the bedding and the carpets.
I'll write down the names for you, and tell you
where you can get them. . .

(Note: The RSPCA can supply these directly
but not the PDSA. At the latter there will have
been some pre-printed sheets with the details of
the treatment, but these will long ago have run
out, and no one will have had the time or energy
to replace them.)

Client: What about tablets? Those things advertised
on TV.

Vet: I'm afraid we don't have those, and you can't get
them from a chemist. We're a charity and we
have limited funds.

At this point the vet reflects on the advantage of
working for a charity. There are many flea treatments
available to the private veterinary client, and it's
exhausting giving a full rundown on the relative
merits and costs of each! Clients never bother to read
the leaflets available in the waiting room.

Foreign Bodies

No topic better illustrates the stupidity of man and beast than this one. There are many types of foreign body, but to keep this section to a reasonable length I shall illustrate the subject with only a few examples of oral, nasal, pedal and gastrointestinal foreign bodies.[33]

Oral foreign bodies
I'm all for exercise, but why do cretins insist on throwing long and sharp sticks for their equally brainless mutts? How often do such sticks, dangling from the mouths of galumphing canids, lodge in the ground, thus ramming the proximal extremities into the depths of the daft creatures' throats? The broken-off tips can be very difficult to find, causing recurrent abscesses and large vet bills. To add insult to injury,[34] the owners will insult the vet at his not being able immediately to locate and remove every tiny fragment of wood deposited at the time of the initial injury, and will probably refuse to pay some of the mounting bill. If the vet is a junior employee,[35] his boss will generally take the owners' side. My advice to young vets in such

---

[33] Of course vets don't generally have to deal with the 'embarrassingly misplaced' objects that doctors do, but that's small compensation.

[34] Notice the clever literal use of this expression. I am trying to extract every little pleasure from writing about these experiences as living them was so miserable.

[35] See Owners' Guide to Vets p109

cases is (a) to warn the owners at the outset (preferably after sucking in air through your teeth and tutting at their explanation of what happened) that they might take a long time to resolve and, (b) to hand them over to the boss as soon as you possibly can.

Nasal foreign bodies
The commonest form of nasal foreign body is the blade of grass lying just above the soft palate of the domestic cat, technically in the 'nasopharynx'. All carnivores eat some vegetable material from time to time and most cats will chew grass. Occasionally such greenery will go astray. The affected moggy will be sneezing and retching and you won't be able to get a good look without administering an anaesthethic.

If you are lucky enough to have suitable instruments then you are a quarter of the way to solving the problem. There's not a lot of room in a cat's throat and you need a laryngoscope to illuminate the scene, an instrument for grasping the grass, and possibly another item to pull the palate back. Sometimes the least touch will move the grass blade forward and out of reach. On other occasions the grass will break off every time you attempt to get hold off it, becoming progressively shorter and more difficult to retrieve as your blood pressure mounts and your boss agitates about how long you are taking over 'such a simple procedure'. Hands trembling and sweat pouring, on one occasion I failed to dislodge the leaf and had to send the cat home. I think it eventually sneezed it out. Bloody cats!

Pedal foreign bodies
I blame litterbugs for many of these incidents, often slivers of broken glass embedded in dogs' paws (al-

71

though, of course, thorns are also common) and this is a good opportunity to rant at these despicable scum.

People who drop litter, smash bottles *etc.* have clearly been failed by their parents, the education system and society in general but I still blame them. I've never seen anyone being arrested for this offence but sometimes have a go at them myself – it's a good way to let off steam after a hard day of attempting to find and remove fragments of glass from dogs' paws. The ill-mannered louts are generally ungrateful for my pointing out the error of their ways. To me such behaviour shows a lack of respect to one's country, the world, animals, other people and oneself. There is no excuse whatsoever for littering, and no punishment could possibly be harsh enough (and the same goes for people who let their dogs foul pavements). On second thoughts, why not force these worthless pieces of human excrement to squeeze anal glands for a living? Yes, let them become vets!

Gastrointestinal foreign bodies

Vet: Good morning, Mr. Grodgeblimp. How are you and Sam [a glaikit [36] Springer Spaniel] today? I hope he's OK. It's not time for his stitches to come out yet, is it?

Client: Errrr, no. . . Ummm. . . You know the stone you removed the other day?

Vet: Yes, I gave it to you in a little packet didn't I? A tricky operation but he should be OK. He looks fine, has he been OK?

Client: Errrr, yes, full of beans.

---

[36] Great Scots word applicable to many pets and their owners.

Vet: You've been keeping him rested I hope? We don't want him running around and jumping yet.

Client: Ah, well. . . It's difficult you know. . .

At this point the vet is beginning to realise what has happened and has an 'Oh shit!' moment.

Vet: Oh no! He's not. . . ? Has he?

Client: I'm afraid so. I was just showing the stone to my wife and before I could do anything Sam jumped up and. . .

This is a true story. Anonymity has been preserved to offer partial protection to the imbecilic owner and his equally unintelligent mutt. Both survived. The vet is getting his revenge now.

Friends

You had a few before you became a vet did you?
Expect to gain 'friends' and lose Friends once you're a
pet repairperson. . .

First off, your social life will necessarily be con-
strained by the nights and weekends working/on-call.

Secondly, you'll not be able to take invitations (to
those few parties you are able to attend) at face value
any more. After the greetings, and the supply of a
drink – which, after your utterly Shih T(zu) day, you'll
need! – your genial host will:

(a) expect you to spend the evening romping with
his slobbering Gordon Setter (making it impossible
for you to eat any of the cocktail snacks unless you
don't mind saliva all over your hands and the dog
standing up against your chest as you munch the *hors
d'oeuvres*);

(b) pump you for advice on the maintenance of his
geriatric cat; and

(c) introduce you to all and sundry as a vet, so
your whole evening will be spent dispensing further
free advice or (worse) listening to insufferably lengthy
and tedious sagas concerning the doings of various
Sachas (incidentally, a male name in Russia and
France. but applied to female animals here!), Trixies
and Tysons – grrr!

Thirdly, 'friends' will expect, at the very least, free vaccinations for their pets. If your boss is understanding he'll let you do these for cost price. . . but if he lets you do them 'for nothing', you will henceforth owe him a debt of gratitude, so that you'll be the one who is 'requested' to work that extra weekend when he wants even more time off. . . The worst possibility is when a friend's animal, under your care (paid for or gratis), fails to recover from some affliction. The 'friend' will seriously doubt your competence, hypocritically thank you for your trouble, and disappear from your life, liberally spreading libellous calumnies.

It's unlikely that you'll muster sufficient courage to tell your 'friends' face-to-face what all these 'little' favours cost you. In the end the resentment will poison your friendships, unless you expunge it by writing a book called *Pet Hates* or, seeing as I've already used that option, by buying a copy for the thoughtless importuning parasites, and ordering them to read this section!

Gastric Dilation/ Volvulus Syndrome[37]

I'm all for ailments that deprive the world of nasty big dogs, provided that tending to the terminating terrors doesn't involve too much unpleasant labour for the vet. Unfortunately, the bloated stomach syndrome invariably does.

The theory is that large deep-chested dogs shouldn't eat huge gas-producing meals and then indulge in vigorous exercise, but there appear to be many people out there who think it an excellent idea for Satan to bolt several bags of dog food pellets at midnight, not having eaten all day, drink two litres of water and then indulge in some Frisbee-chasing. Presently Satan has been converted into a vast gasping football bladder. (If you were trapped in the jungle, and needed a drum to call for help, but only had a Dobermann, a Frisbee, and a sack of dog food. . .)

Back to reality. It isn't the jungle, and the object is to extract money from the cli. . . oops. . . save the life of the pneumato-paunched Pinscher. Satan's gums are now a horrible dirty blue-orange (work that out!). It's very difficult for him to force his diaphragm down against the tumid tummy so he can't take a decent breath, and he is gasping shallowly. None of the blood

---

[37] bloating/twisting of the stomach

that his weak and rapidly beating heart manages to send to the further reaches of his body can return to that failing pump past his vast abdomen – all the veins are squashed flat. The pressure continues to build as the dog food ferments in the heated brewer's vat which the stomach has become. Satan is dying.

The owners (a yuppie childless couple who dote on the pooch) could not be described as serene. You rush around trying to find the stomach tubes. They are not where they should be. You open every drawer and cupboard in the practice. You phone the on-duty nurse. She doesn't know either, but she's on her way over. Ten-to-one an accursed slap-dash large animal vet[38] has borrowed them and left them in his car. In desperation you cut a gas hose free from an oxygen cylinder, lubricate the end, and with the owners' help, slide it down the nearly comatose dog's throat. It won't go into the stomach, try as you might. You try to find a trochar to punch a decompression hole directly through the side of the bloated blimp. No trochar. The large bore needle you resort to just keeps blocking. . .

Sometimes one manages to decompress these cases, flush out the putrid liquor, stabilize them, administer anaesthetic and open them up. Once in a while one can work out what's what and restore the parts to their normal position. Occasionally the stomach wall isn't entirely dead, and one can make repairs and fix things firmly in place. Rarely, they survive this operation. Once in a few years of after-hours work they don't die a day or two later. That's a fair reflection of the stress:satisfaction ratio of the profession.

---

[38] see Large Animal Work p95

Gerbils

Isn't it amazing how people think nothing of setting break-back traps for wild mice and rats, but sob their eyes out when the mortality of their pet rodents becomes evident, and they request a 'humane' over-dose of vitamin P?

No, not at all. People are unthinking hypocrites whose ideas of kindness are illogical in the extreme. Most clients would be grossly offended if one attempted to counter their ridiculous notions, and to persuade them that the kindest way to kill a geriatric gerbil would be to bash its head in with a brick, not to jab it with a needle. Still, that's how one makes one's money.

Your average fit gerbil, in for its claws to be clipped, is a bewhiskered will-o'-the-wisp with fangs. Catching these horrible Houdinis is not only taxing, but also terrifying once you've experienced the sensation of the opposing incisors meeting in your flesh. If one's taken an aspirin in the near past for a stress- and lunch deficiency-induced headache, the wound will bleed for hours, forcing one to consult with a huge blood-soaked dressing wrapped around a finger. Try squeezing an anal gland with that on!

Gratitude

Many people seem to think that vets go home every day basking in the warm glow of satisfaction from a job well done, the grateful words of clients ringing in their ears, a box of chocolates under their arms, and a song on their lips. Not so.

To continue with my task of disabusing the unenlightened: gratitude generally seems to be more forthcoming from those for whom you have done the least, and least forthcoming from those for whose animals you have slaved night and day, personally nursing them even when not officially on duty. It's the old widow on a meagre pension whose poodle you put down a week ago, in a purely automatic fashion, and whom you can't even remember, who sends you a box of chocolates and a card thanking you for '. . . the caring and sensitive way you eased Trixie from this life. . . '

The owner of the pup that survived Parvovirus only because you went in to the practice after 1 am every night for five nights to check and replace the drip, clean up all the excrement *etc.*, will not utter a word of thanks when you hand the now healthy, happy, bouncy creature back, but will complain acrimoniously about the size of the bill. You want to tell the ignorant lout that the cost of the preventive vaccination would have been a fraction of the cost of treatment, but you remain polite and professional as you itemise the bill. The former succeeds in making you feel guilty and inadequate, the latter is aggravating in the extreme.

Give me no more than uniform civility, rather than a mixture of misplaced excessive gratitude and equally inappropriate hostility.

Guinea Pigs

They are not pigs, and they don't come from Guinea, but of all the animals one deals with as a vet they are possibly the least obnoxious. Their owners, however, run the usual gamut. 'I find them delicious!' is the conversational gambit of one chap I know, whenever the topic of these squeaking South American rodents is raised. By contrast, I was roped into presiding at the funeral of one 'Albert', with whom the distraught owner had enjoyed 'a profound spiritual bond'. He was apparently 'the only one who understood' her.

Did I get a warm glow from my gentle presence at the grand ritual, do you think? Was I happy to sacrifice an hour of my precious free time? Can you hear my hysterical laughter?

Aside from when they need their claws clipped, guinea pigs tend to be presented:
(a) with mange (a problem readily resolved by a course of injections but which, left untreated, will see them waste away and die in agonised convulsions due to the maddening itch) or
(b) on the point of death for reasons unknown.

Obviously one can derive a modicum of satisfaction from dealing with the former but the latter phenomenon is the pits, because the brutes expire on the table before one can administer vitamin P (see Euthanasia) thus preventing one from legitimately charging for one's services. Furthermore, the owners then proceed to have full-blown emotional break-downs, reliving all the traumas of their awful pasts.

One has no choice but to muster that sympathetic expression and tone of voice (No. 3 in the veterinary surgeons' stock repertoire), proffer a tissue or five, and grit one's teeth, as seething frustrated masses accumu-late in the waiting room – dogs peeing on the display racks and fighting while snotty-nosed brats wail and smear chocolate over the poor receptionist's desk.

Under such circumstances, how many times can one murmur, 'Unfortunately these things sometimes happen. I'm sure you looked after him well. He obviously didn't suffer for long. He's at peace now. . .' before one goes stark, staring, raving banana-bonkers mad?

Hair

It gets everywhere, not just into the 70s as a musical, but also all over your clothes and car (Yuk!). It also dominates conversations. The two commonest phrases uttered in veterinary practices both concern hair coming off animals, or failing to come off, as the case may be.

The commonest hair sentence uttered by staff is: 'These clippers are useless!' Bosses are generally too penny-pinching and short-sighted to replace old and faulty equipment as often as they should.[39]

The most frequent pelage-related expression of clients is: 'Ooh, isn't she shedding a lot? It's because she's frightened!'

Utter nonsense. The hair's innervation only controls the pilo-erector muscles, and causes such phenomena as the raising of hackles and goose pimples. It's impossible for animals to shed their hair instantly and voluntarily. There are four reasons for people making such inane remarks. The first is to cover their guilt at not grooming their charges. The second is to make pleasant inoffensive small talk. The third is that the state of bestial *chevelure* is particularly apparent under the bright light of the consulting room and against the dark surface of the rubber table top.

---

[39] see A Typical Day on p142 for more on clippers

The fourth is that the animal is invariably being held firmly while it attempts to escape, thus causing cascades of loose hair to fall. So there is indeed a correlation between Sheba being frightened and shedding hair, but not the way the owner thinks!

Believe me, one becomes utterly sick of explaining all this. If one throws in a discussion of the effects of photoperiod, temperature, thyroid hormones and sex steroids on the hair growth cycle your consultation might well last half an hour. The best option in the long run is just to grit your teeth, try to look amused, and get on with the consultation.

Dematting long-haired cats is one of the many tedious tasks best left to nurses. Long-haired cats are almost always foul-tempered beyond imagining, and you'll be completely unable to groom them without at least sedating them heavily. If the owner will allow it you can save yourself (or the nurses) a great deal of time and effort by shaving the animal bald. Why on earth do people breed such monsters?

Hamsters

Although hamsters are not as agile as gerbils, they can still be difficult to apprehend. They are pretty nifty at turning their heads around so as better to position those oral chisels to incise one's fingers. When I have to examine one of them or, for example clip its claws,[40] I prefer to drape a thin cloth or a piece of folded paper over the rodent-in-question's neck. Then – and one has to work quickly here – one attempts to gather all the loose neck skin between one's thumb and forefinger. Due to the cheek pouches there is a great deal of this. I am advantaged here because I am 'double-jointed': I can widely splay the last joints of my thumb and forefinger, enabling me to gather all the skin as I roll them in. At this stage of the proceedings the hamster should be relatively helpless and you can examine it. I should warn you that a hamster suspended like this is not a pretty sight. Indeed, all bulging eyes and teeth, it looks repulsive as it struggles. The little kid who owns it will be crying. Don't hold them too long – they can easily suffocate.

Hamsters are useful for teaching children about mortality. At two-and-half years of age they are living on borrowed time, and they tend to go down with multiple ailments: hair loss, skin infection (a rival to the Parvovirus diarrhoea of dogs for the most obnox-

---

[40] see Nail-clipping p102

ious odour prize!) weight loss, paralysis, trembling, diarrhoea. . . There is little point in treating any of these things, unless it is to milk the client of money. Young hamsters also suffer from diarrhoea, so-called 'wet-tail'. Vitamin P is the only treatment guaranteed to resolve the problem!

Most vets will have anecdotes about hamsters in hibernation, along the lines of clients imagining dead hamsters to be alive or vice versa. The best story I heard was about a hamster lying in a shoebox. The owner had thought it had died, but look! Yes, it was definitely moving: peculiarly undulating its body. The vet picked it up to reveal a seething mass of maggots – problem solved![41]

---

[41] see Rabbits p120 for more about maggots

Heart Failure

Ideally, the treatment of heart failure covers the whole gamut of veterinary science – from the offering of simple advice about exercise restriction, to more complex dietary modification, chest X-rays and ECGs, to multi-drug regimens of labyrinthine complexity and gargantuan expense, and the installation of pacemakers. The difficulty for the perfectionist is knowing at which point on this spectrum to place a particular case. Quite apart from the animal's age and physical condition, the factors to be considered are multiple: the depth of the owner's pockets, the owner's ability to cope with what can be complex information, the practice's policies (if these exist) and what drugs the practice holds in stock, the degree to which you want to eliminate the possibility of after-hours calls, the amount of time available to evaluate and discuss the case (*i.e.* the pressure of other cases), your own moral standpoint and what other vets in the practice have already told the owner. What the owner desires is, of course, ultimately what you do, but to some extent what the owner desires can be manipulated by what you tell him.

As a keen young vet, your primary focus is on the treatment of the physical condition. You explain the physiology to the owner in great depth; you initiate expensive investigations and assessments, and may end up keeping the animal going a few weeks with frequent protracted consultations. The other vets are irritated by your 'time-wasting' as the waiting room backlog grows. They're also embarrassed at having to re-explain all the ins and outs of the complicated regime of treatment on those days when you're not at the surgery; embarrassed because they've all forgotten what the drugs do. Before very long one of them will put the dog down behind your back.

It's not long before you drop all the idealistic thoroughness: furosemide and aminophylline are the only drugs you use, and you hustle the clients and patients in and out of the consulting room as quickly as possible. You might suggest dietary modification if you can be bothered. If the panting patient doesn't respond to these limited means, it's euthanasia. The astute reader will realise that this is the whole of small animal veterinary science in a nutshell. The philosopher-idealist will recognise that this is the whole of life in a nutshell: nothing but filthy compromise and disillusion.

Home Visits

Things are tough at the surgery, but they're so much worse in clients' homes. The strength of insistence of a client on a home visit, the pressure of work at the practice, the difficulty of locating the client's residence, and the ultimate futility of the call are all correlated. I keep thinking I've experienced all the horrors that visits can offer, but I'm still surprised by novel ones.

Visits are very expensive for the client, and with good reason. So why, then, is it often the poorest people in the worst areas who insist on them? (Incidentally, this is one of the few advantages of working for the RSPCA or the PDSA – these bodies recognise that it would be far too dangerous to expect their vets to visit people's homes.) When you've successfully negotiated the drunks in the unsignposted backstreets, obtained directions from stray glue-sniffing kids, and mounted the decaying steps in a urine-scented stairwell, you are only standing on the threshold of a truly insalubrious environment. There is at first no answer when you knock on the door. You wonder if you've come to the right place. You knock again, much louder. Still no reply. You are conscious of all the operations waiting at the surgery, and of the diminishing chances of a lunch break, and you're just about to give up when a weak old voice says, 'Coming!' Several minutes of uninterrupted mumbling follow, accompanied by a repeated clunking sound. Both noises increase in intensity. There is a moment of silence, and you can feel an eye inspecting you through the peephole. The door opens slowly. You are almost knocked off your feet by the most foetid, pungent, gag-inducing stench you've experienced since the last geriatric hamster. An ancient and filthy hag stands there, propped on a walking stick. Over her shoulder hell lies waiting.

You've seen those junk shops, full of ancient commemorative crockery, hideous vases, brass bric-à-brac and mock-Grecian gimcracks? Take a few shopfuls. Add the contents of a bookshop and of a newsagent from the first half of the last century. Add seventeen cats, preferably faeco-urinally challenged, and reproductively intact. Close all windows and doors, and turn up the heating. Mix well and leave to fester for at least forty years. If you can't cut the air with a knife, sprinkle liberally with cat urine and milk, tread some miscellaneous faecal material into the carpet, make the householder incontinent also, and let a few forgotten kittens decompose behind the wardrobe. Now send in a vet.

'Yes, it's Arthur. He's been losing weight. Arthur! Good boy, Arthur. Let the vet look at you, now. He's come to help you. Still, Arthur!'

Arthur, patchily both bald and matted, skeletal and pyorrhoeic (drooling blood and pus) somehow manages to hiss and scuttle off into the nether regions of the house. To your eyes, he might well be one of the fittest cats here.

'Oh, dear. Would you like a cup of tea, dear? Poor dear, he's terrified.'

You wonder if she's talking about you or the cat, as you decline the tea, 'I'm afraid time is short, Mrs. X, I really must be getting back to the surgery. Let's see if we can catch Arthur. . . '

'Eh? Oh, no, don't chase him. He'll be under the bed. Wait for him to come out. . . '

But, driven by your desperation to get out as quickly as possible, you go and grope around in the stinking Stygian netherworld. With your fingertips, you can just reach the skulking seborrhoeic vestige of a cat. By thrusting (your face comes into contact with the cat hair- and excreta-caked carpet) you manage to get a grip, and you haul out the epitome of catabolic crisis, suffering only minor injuries because the claws are all ingrown, and the mouth is too sore to be used for any purpose other than spluttering exudate.

'Don't hurt him! He's not been eating well for the last few weeks.'

'Has he been drinking a lot?' You have learnt to shout by this stage.

'Eh? Drinking? Oh, yes, he's been drinking very well!'

'Well, I'm afraid, despite that, he's very dehydrated. I say, he's very dehydrated. His kidneys are tiny. I have to be honest with you. He's suffering from severe kidney failure. His kidneys are not working! At this stage there's no hope. I really think the kindest thing would be to put him down! I say the kindest thing is to put him down!'

'Oh, don't do that. The last vet said that fish would be good for him!'

'Yes, but you've just told me that he isn't eating, and he won't be with a mouth like that. All the poisons that the kidneys should get rid off are coming out in his saliva and rotting his mouth. If he's drinking a lot then he's already helping his kidneys as much as he can. . . '

'The other vet says I should give him fish. I've been heating it like he said. . . '

At this point you decide to cut your losses and leave. 'I tell you what I'll do, I'll give him an injection to build his strength up, and some vitamins and some antibiotics for his mouth. I'll also give you some powder to mix in his water. . . '

Self-extrication takes longer than you'd thought as there are more ultra-decrepit animals to be seen (only one was mentioned when she phoned for a visit). It's such a relief to get out that you don't even notice which way you're driving and you end up going the wrong way on a one-way system. You are already late for afternoon consultations, never mind the morning's operations. . . and lunch?![42]

Variations on the above scenario are fairly common. So too are variations on the small-hours visit to a gloomy chamber in an obscure and distant suburb where a huge and ancient dog lies dying surrounded by mourning masses. It's too dark to see anything (one often has to ask for someone to hold a torch), there's no room to work and the dog's blood pressure is very low, so it's sweatful work trying to find a vein in front of the huge keyed-up audience. If one's lucky enough to be able to break away from post-euthanasia counsel-

---

[42] see Lunch p101

ling (it's useful to trigger one's pager!) the next task is to lug the massive hound out with as much dignity as possible.

It's always a quandary whether to bag the dog[42] in front of the owners or not, because there's no way to do this in a manner which seems respectful. Usually one requests a blanket and carts the carcass out wrapped in this. Of course this won't be sufficient to prevent it leaking over one's clothes and in one's car. If one only has a short journey it's sufficient to lay the dog on top of some plastic bags, but if it's a long bumpy ride this won't prevent the car becoming mucky and the smell permeating everything.

In this case the best thing to do is to drive around the corner, and attempt to bag the body single-handed. Have you ever been spotted by the police as you struggle to put an enormous excrement-smeared Rottweiler into a relatively small plastic bag on the verge of a suburban road at 2.34 am? ('Honestly, Constable, I'm just doing my job!') This has happened to me, in a seedy part of Greater Manchester, although I couldn't swear to the exact time.

---

[42] see Corpses p44

Large Animal Work

For practical purposes large animal work can be divided into farm animal and equine work. If you want to become a farm animal vet, the first thing you have to do is jettison all those soppy ideas about reducing suffering. Farm animals are nothing but economic units to the farmer, and if humane modifications to the time-honoured brutal rituals of large animal husbandry add to the cost or duration of the procedures, forget it. The farmer will not call you again. Oh, you want to reduce suffering by improving the efficiency of the whole set-up, to prevent problems rather than patch them up by doing the romantic fire brigade stuff? (After all, the latter becomes a pain in the **** after the first few weeks of adrenalin highs!)

Unfortunately for you, farmers fall into two categories: those who know everything already, rendering you and your bright-eyed, bushy-tailed new-graduate ideas for herd health schemes redundant, and those who know nothing and have no intention of learning anything. . . ever. So there!

Working with horses. . . Ah, the very phrase conjures images of the rural idyll: leaning on the railings of a paddock watching an attractive young filly putting an attractive young filly through her paces, while you nod sagely in your tweed jacket, sucking on your briar pipe, kindly eyes twinkling. The snorting horse is pulled up for you to examine. Your firm masculine hands unerringly locate the source of the problem. The radiantly grateful brown eyes of the jodhpur-clad vision meet yours, 'Oh, Mr Artmeier, I'm so grateful. Is there anything I can do for you?'

Her breasts heave beneath her taut T-shirt, and her soft warm hands clasp yours and squeeze meaning-fully. You fall into the tropical island dream of those wonderful eyes. . . BEEP, BEEP, BEEP! Your pager has just gone off. You were dreaming. You're not dreaming now. It's another damned colic at Trashbrook Stables. The brute's been ill all day, and they call at 3 am! Why don't they worm their horses, or feed them properly? They've been cutting costs and now if the horse dies it'll be your fault. It's a bloody expensive showjumper too. The owner has come out. Utterly hysterical, of course. The horse bleeds like stink when you pass the naso-gastric tube. Joy.

Horse owners are obnoxious. They are notoriously snobbish, conceited and full of themselves, particu-larly the *nouveaux riches*. Consequently, if you're into smarm and flattery, you can become a very successful equine vet. You don't need to know much, just look and sound knowledgeable, and, for heaven's sake, agree with the client! The rich are often wealthy by virtue of their reluctance to part with money, so expect delayed payment and threats of malpractice suits and the like.

There are some advantages to being a large animal

vet. You get a rest from people and animals as you drive between farms. Never mind the fact that your chances of having a car accident are high, these breaks, during which you can listen to your favourite music (or 'get lost' down a shady lane – don't use this excuse too often!), mean that your diurnal stress levels will be lower than those of the full-time small animal vet, who's in the the thick of it all virtually non-stop. At night, it's a different story of course, especially during the birthing season!

Oh. . . nearly forgot to mention that as agriculture is in decline, farmers are less and less inclined to call out the vet. This has two consequences. Firstly, practices are having to cover larger and larger geographical areas, making nights on-call a veritable marathon driving nightmare. Secondly, a major source of income is the sale of drugs, worm medicines and the like, and farmers are becoming ever more astute at playing practices off against each other to get the best deals. I have warned you! Again!

Locums

The word comes from the Latin *locum tenens*, literally 'holding the place' (of someone who is absent) *i.e.* this is short-term employment covering for permanent staff on holiday and the like. There are advantages and disadvantages to being a locum vet.

The main advantage is that if a particular practice is awful one only has to tolerate it for a short period. Additional advantages include the fact that one is, to a large extent, spared the trauma of hero worship by clients; it is possible to refer most of the problematic long-term cases to a permanent vet. One can similarly avoid most difficult operations – a locum is seldom expected to perform these. As one is well paid it's possible to take two months holiday out of every three months (assuming one is single, and without dependants or a Porsche to support!). However, expect to suffer during that one month of work!

As one is only in a practice for at most a few weeks, one is constantly having to learn new geographies, hierarchies, and working practices. No two practices are identical in their structures (though the personality problems are often similar). They vary from small single-branch practices with only one or two vets (easy to learn the system but horribly claustrophobic if one doesn't see eye-to-eye with other personnel), through medium practices with one main surgery and one or two small satellite branches (in some ways the nicest practices to work for as the small branches give one some breathing space without giving one an undue amount to learn in a short time) to huge organisations with at least two main surgeries and multiple satellites.

The latter practices are very stressful to work for as invariably the main surgeries constitute mutually hostile camps run on entirely different and incompatible lines. You will be caught in the crossfire of wilfully misunderstood messages and obstructionism. You will perform Task A according to the rules of Surgery 2 while at Surgery 1, and be upbraided accordingly. You will at first be amused and flattered to be the confidential safety valve, and be told all the faults of X, Y and Z by Q, and all the faults of Q, R and S by X, but eventually you'll want to strangle the lot of them – miserable whingers! If they don't like the situation why don't they get out!? That's the $64,000 question.[43]

As a locum you'll often be in the position of picking up the pieces of grossly mismanaged cases. Just what do you say to the client if your new treatment resolves a case which has been treated unsuccessfully for months (*e.g.* severe anaemia caused by a massive flea infestation – Serengeti-wildebeest loads of them! – entirely missed by the vet you're replacing who'd suspected chronic intestinal bleeding)? How

---

[43] see Advice for Would-Be Veterinarians p151

can you avoid leaving the client with the impression that his vet is incompetent? Does this constitute unprofessional conduct, or is it more unprofessional to continue mismanaging the case? What will the permanent vet (your boss!) think if he returns from his holiday to discover all his long-term money generators cured and many of his clients turned against him?

The automatic defence mechanism of such people is to scrutinize all your work in a desperate attempt to discover some dirt on you. If you're not aware of how to play this game (let the animal suffer for a few more weeks, and suggest the correct treatment very tactfully to the returning permanent vet, whom you know damn well will ignore your advice!), things can degenerate into a bitter series of accusations and counter-accusations.

Thus, there is a difference between being a successful locum (*i.e.* recommended and re-employed) and a good practitioner. Like every other aspect of veterinary practice, if one thinks about it too much one's emotional wellbeing is threatened.

I shudder as I write this.

Lunch

Ha, ha, ha! You poor ignorant fool!

Nail Clipping

Along with spaying bitches, and vaccinating dogs
against kennel cough, this is probably the most
difficult thing a vet has to do. As a rule, animals loathe
having their nails clipped and owners are incapable of
holding them still, even if you very patiently demon-
strate. Call a nurse in to help you if there's one in a
good mood available (admittedly unlikely). Or, better
still, send the owner away with a handful of tranquillisers to shove down his recalcitrant dog's throat
before a repeat appointment. If the animal has dark
claws always warn the owner of the possibility of
bleeding as you won't necessarily be able to see or
avoid the quick, and always have ferric chloride or
potassium permanganate handy to stem the haemor-
rhage. The latter is less likely to leave your finger tips
stained black.

If it's a cage bird you'll have to hold it yourself. Put
a block of wood in your mouth so that you can bite on
it when the bird pinches the delicate skin at the
margins of your fingernails – excruciating doesn't
begin to describe it – and don't forget to warn the
owner of the possibility of his feathery friend expiring
as soon as you touch it.

Nurses. . .
and Would-Be Nurses

Here's what I thought of them until I met a few damn good ones recently:

Many start as school drop-outs, who've 'always loved animals'.[44] The brightest ones leave quickly, once they realise what nursing entails. The semi-bright go on to get a qualification, then become increasingly bitter as the horrible truth about their job dawns. Most practices pay them peanuts, and use them as glorified skivvies. The bulk of even a qualified nurse's work would bore and frustrate a hamster. Why train these people at all if one doesn't use their skills?

The upshot of this is that nurses become horribly sour and resentful, unwilling to perform the least exceptional task. They function like robots, brains switched off as they mop up excrement and pack drapes, discussing diets while they gorge on chocolates and complain. Complain, did I say? Whinge, moan, fume without cessation. Veterinary nurses epitomise the British disease of ineffectual grumbling. As an assistant or locum veterinarian,[45] you'll have to listen to the same tales of exploitation hundreds of times over. (Or worse, if you're a new graduate some of the

---

[44] see Cat Lovers p35
[45] see Locums p98

nurses might attempt to relieve their frustrations by making your life miserable. They can destroy your self-confidence and reputation as easily as they intrigue against each other.)

Suggest they actually do something about their miserable lot, such as compile a systematic list of their complaints and take it to the management, and they'll look at you as if you're mad! If they all put their names to the document, management would have to give it serious consideration, but none will have the courage to do this. They'll all sit there meekly at staff meetings, seething beneath the surface but speechless, as they are criticised for sloppiness, bad telephone technique or whatever. The atmosphere in a practice – never good – is execrable in the days that follow one of these pathetic charades.

So what changed recently? Well, I met a few who had been treated as human beings by their employers. Makes a big difference.

Obesity

Most so-called 'small' animals aren't. They're GROSSLY overweight. (Some are so fat one is tempted to suggest that the owner covers them with green baize and attaches pockets to the corners – if the dog's too heavy to play games at least it could serve as a snooker table.)

The issue of obesity typifies the paradoxical situation of veterinary science. Vets are paid to treat sick animals, so it's in a vet's interests to keep her charges in a constant state of poorliness. At least when it comes to obesity you can give all the correct advice (which if followed would result in a happy healthy animal), confident in the knowledge that the client will not comply. Your conscience will be clear but the cash will keep rolling in, as the idiot of an owner uses the low-calorie dog food you supply to supplement his pet's normal ration of fillet steak, liver and chocolate. More food will inflate the waddling 'Lard-rador' as the owner wraps the arthritis tablets in slices of ham to get them down.

Here's a typical obesity consultation (edited to a tolerable length):

Vet: What's the problem today then?

As if she doesn't know! Both the owner and the dog are grotesquely elephantine.

Client: Sally's lame.

As this point the vet makes a token attempt to examine the animal, knowing full well that the dog will be suffering from severe degenerative arthrosis of the hips and stifles, and bilateral cruciate ligament rupture, all secondary to carrying twice as much weight as it should.

Vet: She has severe arthritis in her hips and knees.

Note: There's no point explaining the difference between arthritis and arthrosis.

Vet: It's not really surprising. She's very overweight.

Client: I know but I only feed her once a day! She's been spaded [sic], you see, and she only gets very little.

Vet: (Mentally sighing, and gritting her teeth.) What do you feed her?

Client: She won't eat dog food. She gets a little bit of liver, or some steak. It's very little really.

Vet: OK. Well, first of all, most overweight dogs I see are only fed once a day. In fact I think it's worse to feed one relatively big meal than two small ones. You can either starve your dog completely for weeks on end, giving her a vitamin-mineral supplement, or you can feed her a couple of very small meals a day, but then you must give her a balanced diet. What you're giving her is very high in protein and vitamin A. It's not good for her at all. The fact that she's been spayed is not an excuse. She needs less food now than she did before the operation so all you have to do is feed her less.

Client: But she won't eat dog food at all!

Vet: Good. Then that's exactly what you must offer
her. In fact find a dog food she detests and
offer her a small amount of that twice a day. If
she doesn't wolf it down immediately then
take it away. She's not going to starve herself
to death! If she doesn't want a good balanced
food then it's because her body is telling her
she doesn't need to eat any more. What you're
doing is giving her something especially tasty.
Have you seen the Monty Python film, *The
Meaning of Life?* There's a scene in that where
a man has just had a huge meal, and the only

extra thing he'll eat is a 'wafer theen meent', because it tastes so delicious! Then he explodes. What you're giving your dog is the equivalent of the 'wafer theen meent'!

The owner looks very unconvinced, so the vet changes tack.

Vet: There's one more approach. If you'd like to try diet dog food. . . here's a leaflet that goes with it. The nurses run obesity clinics where you can have your dog weighed. If you want to make an appointment or get some diet dog food then go to the reception. In the meantime I'll give Sally some tablets. . .

The vet knows that the only thing she'll ever succeed in lightening is the owner's wallet, so why the hell not!?

Owners' Guide to Vets

For practical purposes there are only four categories of veterinary surgeon in general practice:

(1) The nervous new graduate.

(2) The stressed-out wreck (probably a drug addict or alcoholic), generally suffering from suicidal thoughts.

(3) The in-it-purely-for-the-money shyster.

(4) The balanced, healthy, happy and competent practitioner.

The balanced vet

Let us deal with these in reverse order, and get the last category out of the way first, as balanced and happy vets are rare indeed. Having read a good bit of this book, the question you are no doubt dying to ask is: what explains the miraculous existence of such people? There are two possible answers, not necessarily exclusive.

Firstly, it is likely that they are not academically brilliant and that they only just made it into veterinary school and then scraped through. Brighter people will not find general practice in the least fulfilling, but duller individuals, provided they like people and are equipped with emotional intelligence and extraordinary patience can just about hack it. They will not agonise about the morality of the job. [46]

---

[46] I suggest you refer to the Cat Lovers (p35) section to understand this point.

Secondly, it is almost certain that they will have outside interests and will not work long hours! It is essential to have passions outside of the profession if one is to survive. One vet I know, besides being an avid twitcher (unrelated to alcohol intake), took up pole-vaulting in his late forties. Another takes part in amateur dramatics where she regularly cross-dresses and gets to kiss people. Perhaps the most balanced example of this rare breed enjoys doing shifts as a nightclub bouncer, teaches judo, 'controls' red deer (somewhat lethally), plays extremely loud guitar in a rock band, and takes people fishing – there's nothing like a bit of violence, brutality and torture to help one cope with the stresses of the job!

Because these vets are generally competent and balanced, as an owner you won't have any cause to complain about them. Neither is there any way of riling them for a bit of sport, unless, of course, their extramural activities lend themselves to blackmail.

The shyster
These are generally middle-aged men. You'll recognise them for their jollity, bonhomie and marvellous petside manner. Most owners worship the ground these despicable fraudsters walk on. (This is a major annoyance for those of us who take the investigation and treatment of ailments seriously.) They've usually been in charge of their own practices for some time, and may well have had a string of new graduates as assistants, none of whom stays long once they've seen behind the hail-fellow-well-met mask.

The charlatan won't spend a great deal of time actually examining your pet but will make a positive diagnosis virtually instantly while gabbing on about your favourite sport or whatever other topic particularly interests you. Amazingly, whatever is supposedly wrong with your animal, the treatment will be the same (often a pre-prepared cocktail in a syringe). These vets are inordinately fond of corticosteroids, and they often inject useless vitamins. Invariably your poor (but not necessarily genuinely poorly) pet will have to go back for repeat injections. The bill will be hefty indeed.

Fortunately, as an owner it is ridiculously easy and entertaining to expose and humiliate these old crooks. Simply ask what the precise rationale behind any treatment is, and, for good measure, what the pharmacological mechanism of action is.[47] You might also ask to check the expiry dates on the ancient bottles on the shelves, or enquire as to whether he is complying with the Royal College of Veterinary Surgeons' CPD recommendations.[48] Requesting a second opinion will put the wind up him, as will asking for a transcript of your pet's veterinary record.

If it is not practical for you to go to another practice then make sure you get your pet checked by the seemingly nervous and incompetent new graduate he is employing. Ninety-nine times out of a hundred your pet will be far more thoroughly examined, and you will get an honest opinion. If the young vet seems hesitant then it might well be because a definite diagnosis is not always possible, whatever the genial old codger wants you to believe. Another thing... if a vet looks something up during a consultation then

---

[47] How the drug works, stupid!
[48] Continuing Professional Development (*i.e.* is he keeping up-to-date?)

this a good sign – care is being taken – it's not an indication of incompetence!

I cannot leave this topic without alluding to the fact that these beaming bluffers are usually cunning and psychopathic bullies who treat their staff abysmally. You might sidle up to a veterinary nurse – if he employs such – and ask, on behalf of your 'friend's daughter who is thinking of becoming a veterinary nurse[49] what her typical weekly pay and hours are. If there's no one else around also ask her what it's like working for 'the lovely Mr. X'. Watch her face closely. The truth will be revealed.

The stressed-out wreck

This is how most of us end up. . . well, until we die or commit suicide. If you think I am joking then do some research. You'll find that the profession in the UK has a suicide rate four times that of the average, and twice that of doctors and dentists. This last statistic proves that it is not simply a question of access to lethal drugs. No, it's the awful nature of the job, explained at length in this book. Alcoholism is rife, as is bullying, and my first 'permanent' job[50] was to replace a vet who'd slipped into drug abuse. Within a few weeks, tormented mercilessly by the chief nurse and exhausted by the long hours,[51] I understood why he'd gone off the rails and forgave him the needle-strewn flat. I think I reached my lowest point one evening when, after a gruelling day dealing with obnoxious

---

[49] I've only met one male veterinary nurse during all my years of practice.

[50] What fool could seriously undertake a 'permanent' veterinary job?

[51] For only £10,400 a year, from which I was repaying a loan and paying for my life-saving booze!

owners and unpleasant colleagues, I was doing my official track-veterinarian shift at the local greyhound stadium. One of the dogs ran unusually fast [52] and so I was required to collect a sample to check if it had been doped. The dog's owner refused permission for invasive testing which ruled out a quick and easy blood sample – I had to wait for the dog to urinate. I still have nightmares about that evening.

The punters have all gone home. It is raining. Three men (the track security official, the dog handler and myself) follow a dog around. One of the men clutches a bowl and is near dead with fatigue. He cannot go home until the wretched brute empties its bladder. His eyes widen with horror at the realisation that his life, at that moment, is at the mercy of a mutt's decision to pee.

That was the point at which the seed of this book was planted. This was only the second job of my veterinary career, and already I was fully endarkened[53] as to what the job was really about. Within a brief seven years[54] of this incident I had written the first draft of this book and sent it off. Why the ★★★★ did it take publishers so long to pick up on it? I could have been saved another ten years of misery, depression and anal-gland hell!

Glad that's out of my system. . .

Anyway, as a boss, how do you recognise these broken casualties of the 'wonderfully rewarding

---

[52] Or slow – I've blanked out some of the details of that awful evening.

[53] Somehow 'enlightened' seems the wrong word.

[54] You try finding the time and energy to write after a day of vetting!

profession'? Well, obvious signs are obvious,[55] but some vets are clever at covering up and bully subordinates into complicity. The chances are that if your vet doesn't fit very obviously into one of the other categories, then he or she is in this one. Erratic mood and behaviour, dark circles under the eyes? – put two and two together! I challenge anyone to disprove it.

Once identified, how do you, as an owner, get most enjoyment from your interactions with this category of vet? Well, it seems almost a pity to push over the teetering house of cards constituted by such hopeless cases and their pathetic fabrications, and I don't encourage it – talk about shooting fish[56] in a barrel! But precipitating a crisis would probably be doing them a favour, provided you can get them some professional help before they top themselves. I suggest you hand them a copy of this book with the next paragraph circled and appropriately individualised:

> Get help now! I know you are an alcoholic/
> druggie/suicidally depressed/_____.
> I don't want to report you and get you struck off
> but I will, unless you call one of these helpline
> numbers and sort yourself out: + 44 (0)1926
> 315119 and + 44 (0) 7659 811118.[57]

---

[55] Needle marks on the arms, marked tremor, the reek of booze, rope marks around the neck.

[56] Incidentally, don't expect your average vet to know anything about fish, although I can give you a good recipe for smoked-haddock kedgeree.

[57] The author wishes it known that he receives no money when these numbers are dialled.

If, however, you do wish to be particularly cruel, then circle this also:

> P.S. Sacha's dragging her backside.
> Could she have worms? [58, 59]

The new graduate

When a fresh-faced young vet stands in front of you, stethoscope proudly draped and bursting with hard-won knowledge he is almost heart-breakingly desperate to apply, the best thing you can say is: 'May I see the vet, please?' When the crestfallen reply comes (something along the lines of: 'But I am a vet. Mrs. Frithwick has just employed me. . .') you should snort disparagingly. Then grudgingly let the poor devil examine your pet, throwing in such comments as: 'Mrs. Frithwick doesn't do it like that!/ Be careful, no wonder he's upset!/He's never bitten Mrs. Frithwick.'

When the diagnosis is tentatively offered, and further investigation or treatment suggested, you should snort again and say: 'But Mrs. Frithwick always gives him little white pills and they work fine!' [60]

You may think that such an approach to new graduates amounts to wilful cruelty, but the sooner

---

[58] The vet will think: 'Of course it's not worms, you idiot! Yet another pair of stinking anal glands to squeeze! And Sacha's a male name, you appalling pig-ignorant cretin! Aaaargh!' It'll push him over the edge there and then. (See Anal Glands p18)

[59] In case you're worrying about him reading the previous footnote and thus not believing that it's a genuine request, fear not – he won't have the eyesight or concentration to do so. Another thing: I advise you to leg it after depositing the book on the table!

[60] See Steroids p127

they realise what a catastrophic mistake they have made in their choice of profession, the sooner they will set about investigating alternatives, and the fewer years of their lives will be wasted. If you are worried about pushing them to the brink, well don't be, because you will only be treating them the same way as most other clients – why should you bear responsibility for the suicide? You could also argue that if these naive youngsters plan to stay in the profession then the sooner they toughen up the better. Have fun!

Parvovirus

From the very big to the very small, the name means exactly that: very small virus. This is one of the smallest organisms with which a vet has to contend, but one of the most important. Although it's an important pathogen in a number of species, the effects in dogs are particularly dramatic.

Very few unvaccinated dogs will escape this little bugger, which means that the summer months working for charity organisations are hellish: few of their clientele will ever go to the expense of having their beloved pets vaccinated, and during hot dry spells the virus sits around on pavements and in parks forever. This is one of the most resistant viruses there is, and only the strongest and most unpleasant of disinfectants will kill it.

If you are to effectively sterilise your veterinary surgery you should be using such disinfectants regularly. Unfortunately most practices seem to equip every room with a spray bottle which generates a noxious fine mist every time it is used. Consequently one can tell if a small animal vet is hygiene-conscious by the presence or absence of red eyes and sneezing.

Don't trust a healthy-looking small animal vet – apart from shirking her after-hours work she'll deliberately be leaving her room germ-ridden to foster disease transmission and boost profits!

The typical Parvo patient is a pathetic and disgusting creature indeed. The lining of its entire gastro-intestinal tract jets from both ends, with a good admixture of rotting blood. The smell defies description. If you're lucky you can foist the basic nursing of these poor animals onto the nursing staff.

But there'll always be the 1am visit to the surgery to attend something else, when you notice that the entire area around the Parvo patient's cage is coated with excrement and, what's more, the drip has stopped. Your conscience will force you to attend to it and clean up the mess. Even if you use gloves the smell will attach itself to you, and despite scrubbing yourself raw you won't be able to sleep that night for the stink of it. The dog will of course die anyway, and next year the same owner's replacement puppy will come in for a repeat of the whole dreadful business.

Vaccination[61] costs money, but treatment by the charity organisation you work for is free or laughably cheap.

---

[61] see p133

Pyometras

Abscesses and anal glands, fleas, Parvovirus and pyometras, the dreadful litany of mundane conditions which make up the bulk of a small animal veterinarian's work. . . Thank goodness I've come to the last of these now!

Pyometra means 'pus womb', like Parvovirus this common affliction is easily prevented, in this case by spaying at an early age. Unfortunately ignorant 'animal lovers' prefer not to spend £80 on a simple operation on a six-month-old pup, and end up spending £300 on a pyometra operation, complete with drip, and £175.26 on operations to remove breast cancer (funny how the figures work out like that!).

There are two main categories of pyometra: open and closed. In the former, bloody pus pours from the vulva. In the latter it just builds up inside. Typically the affected bitch is off her food and drinking copiously a few weeks after her last season. If one is lucky the womb is big enough to find easily, but small enough to pull out of the abdomen without rupturing. Large pyometras can contain litres of pus, and sometimes the womb has already burst by the time one enters the abdomen – rather unpleasant!

Once one has hauled the offending organ out, it's traditional to give it to a rookie–nursling to play with. If it's still intact she'll get great pleasure from rupturing it, and squirting the pus out, like some obscene water pistol.

Rabbits

Most practices possess a hapless dupe, known as 'the rabbit expert', to whom all these creatures can be referred. The public image of 'bunnies' is of soft, cuddly, benign, vegetarian children's pets. Some of them are relatively inoffensive, yes, but a large frightened rabbit is certainly not to be sneezed at,[62] far less examined for dental problems! Fearful scarring can result from the raking claws of a lagomorph intent on escape, and as the screaming fury bounces off the walls, you'll have to contend with the wails of the distressed infant owner as well. Wear a long-sleeved jacket and ear-plugs.

The most common rabbit problems are overgrown teeth, associated eye infections and abscesses, maggot infestations (fly strike), and earmite infestations. (Dental problems may be hereditary, but a major factor is a diet too high in pelleted food and various 'treats': rabbits require the abrasive effect of grass and hay to keep their constantly growing teeth worn down.) If the rabbit can be held still, it's easy enough to clip overgrown incisors, but be sure to close your eyes as the ivories go flying! (It's better to burr them with a dental drill but this takes longer and such equipment may not be to hand.) If the molars are

---

[62] Unless you're allergic to rabbit fur, which about one-in-four nurses appear to be.

affected, you'll need to administer a general anaesthetic, from which it might not recover. This is a problematic job as the mouth is small and access is consequently very difficult. You'll probably find that the practice you work for doesn't possess any tools adequate for filing or removing rabbit molars. Send a nurse out to buy a nail file.

In the summer months you'll lift many a rabbit's scut to find a writhing mass of maggots. If it's far gone, it's a case of good old vitamin P deficiency. If it's not too bad, you'll have to pick them all off, clean the excrement-caked fur, and apply suitable insecticidal treatment to all the noisome crevices. The same rabbit will be back two weeks later with the same problem. Don't expect the owners to look after it. That's your job, after all.

Receptionists

Veritable saints. Invariably women between 35 and 60 years old, they bear the brunt of everyone's frustrations. Clients are rude to them. Vets emerge from the nether regions of the practice to harass them about the non-appearance of so-and-so, or the fact that X has a single appointment but has brought three multiply ailing brutes.

They are treated abominably by their employers but somehow feel a deep loyalty to the practice, and they cope with it all. I can only assume that they get some sort of emotional payoff from being everyone's mother substitute, or perhaps it's that sad old story that feminists have tried to combat for so long: the male (husband/boyfriend/boss) destroys the self-esteem of the female so that she feels herself lucky to keep her current position (wife/girlfriend/drudge), and won't dare ask for a rise, or – heaven help us – threaten to resign (separation/divorce).

Don't believe it, women! You're wonderful! I repeat the admonition I made in the section on bosses: stand up for yourselves and let the bastards stew in their own nasty juices!

Skin Problems

Read the sections on fleas, antibiotics and steroids, and you've got a fair idea of what's involved with most dermatological cases. Most skin problems start with fleas. Most vets under-treat dermatological phenomena with antibiotics, and over-treat with steroids. Any lumps should be whipped off.

As a non-specialist there's little more you need to know, perhaps a little about yeast and fungal infections, and mite infestations (why the hell has the useful distinction between 'infection' and 'infestation' been eroded?!) and the fact that most peculiar skin conditions in cats will respond to hormonal treatment. This hormonal treatment has the added advantage that the cats will develop obesity and diabetes – more money!

Anything which fails to respond immediately to such shotgun treatment regimes should be referred to a skin specialist, who'll charge the client a fortune and possibly also be unable to treat it (especially if it's a West Highland White Terrier – on no account ever recommend that anyone ever gets one of these walking repositories of intractable chronic skin disease!), but at least the client won't blame you, and then you can shrug and lift your hands in the air, saying, 'Well, if the skin specialist can't do anything!' as you reach for the good old steroids again. It's all so satisfying.

Spaying

The most under-estimated routine operation of all. Simple enough in young slim small bitches, the operation becomes a nightmare in obese middle-aged Rottweilers and the like. Strictly speaking, in pulling up the ovaries you should break their suspensory ligaments to improve the exposure. That's the theory. In practice, in obese animals the blood vessels often rupture at this point. There's nothing worse than groping through a mess of grease and blood trying to locate a bleeder! It's time to call in another vet, or a nurse, to hold all the gunk out of the way. Personally, I refuse to spay obese bitches. Not only is the operation fiendishly difficult, but if the owner can't keep his animal's weight down before the operation, he's not going to manage afterwards!

Specialists

You might suppose that one guaranteed way out of the stressful yet stultifying tedium of veterinary practice would be to specialise. You'd be forgiven for supposing this – many desperate vets do. Lacking the courage to admit to themselves what a mistake they made in becoming vets, and not having the gumption to start again in some other field, they fool themselves into believing that by obtaining a certificate in some specialisation their lives will instantly become so much richer and more worthwhile. Ha, ha!

The first problem they'll have is finding enough interesting cases to write up. If anyone else in the practice is doing a certificate there'll be a throat-cutting competition for such rarities. Secondly, at the end of an exhausting day of going through such charades as the obesity and flea consultations and so forth, it'll take extraordinary willpower to hit the books. Thirdly, very often the owners of sought-after material won't be particularly keen to disburse vast sums for the work-up and treatment. Panicking about the deadline for the certificate, the would-be specialist will thus often do these cases for virtually nothing.

At this point warning bells should be ringing: what are the chances of deriving any long-term satisfaction out of all the extra knowledge if one is unlikely to be able to use it? However, most people who stick veterinary science for long enough to be specialising have perfected the art of self-deception to the extent that they have become deaf to such warning bells. In their heads they have a picture of this Elysian existence: 'Ahhh, what have we got to do today? Three interesting referrals! Should be able to fit in a round of golf this afternoon. . . and perhaps a visit to the car show-rooms. My daughter fancies a Porsche for her seventeenth birthday. Hmmmn. Might just stretch to that. Now, where were those holiday brochures?'

In reality, they'll still be squeezing anal glands *etc*. from 9 am to 7 pm for the bulk of their income, only now their useless but hard-won new knowledge will be consuming their souls in fires of bitter frustration.

To the non-specialist, specialists are a godsend. You can refer all your problem clients to such people. Merely offering to refer them often gets the most obnoxious whingers to shut up. In effect, you are taking all the wind out of their sails by admitting that you do not have an instant solution – they can no longer enjoy the game of trying to prove your incompetence. If they want to take things further you have given them that option. They won't want to once they discover how much it'll cost, and they won't complain again. It's known as calling their bluff.

Steroids

Oh, those little white pills! Never mind the Olympics or the Tour de France, one could write volumes about steroid abuse in veterinary practice, but it wouldn't be anabolic steroids one would be talking about.

Corticosteroids are wonderful at relieving inflammation and itchiness.[63] They're great at lowering fevers, and getting inappetant animals to eat. They also shoot the immune system to hell. They thin the skin, they cause balding, and they weaken the muscles. They produce potbellies, and polydipsia (excessive drinking) and predispose to diabetes.

Oh yes, they temporarily relieve the symptoms of arthritis, but what happens to the animal's weight, and the joint cartilage in the long run? (Sorry, in the short and painful crawl!)

As a locum, or as a novice veterinarian, you will encounter these long-term steroid junkies, and you will explain the side effects to the owner and attempt to wean the animals off the 'preds'. The vet who initiated the course will be furious. The short-term withdrawal symptoms will convince the owner that his dog needs them, and your idealism will suffer yet another blow.[64]

---

[63] see Fleas p66
[64] see Ethics and Motivation p58

Tablets

Counting out tablets is an enervating task which, if you're lucky, you can delegate to nursing staff. If you are unlucky you'll be up to the hundred-and-some-thing-th tablet when the client will ask a question, and you'll lose count and have to start again. Or, worse still, when you've spent ages explaining the intricacies of heart failure and its treatment to a client, worked out dosages and counted out handfuls of diuretics, bronchodilators, vasodilators, angiotensin converting enzyme inhibitors, cardioglycosides and antibiotics[65] for his past-it pooch, he'll decide to have it put down instead. [66]

[65] see Antibiotics p21
[66] see Euthanasia p61

Teeth

Dogs are descended from wolves. Wolves' teeth are used to tear whole moose into swallowable chunks (remember that Volvos are built like tanks to withstand moose!). Wolves do not have significant dental problems. Dogs are fed soft mush from cans, or tiny dried pellets from packets. Dogs suffer severe dental problems. Surprise, surprise!

More or less ditto for cats: wild and feral cats' dental equipment must reduce birds, rabbits and rodents to swallowable chunks. Pet cats don't need teeth at all to consume the slop they're fed. They are fed gunk because pet owners are gullible, and pet food manufacturers are clever. A tin packed with whole rats and birds would not appeal to the average 'cat lover',[67] whose warped morality compels him rather to stuff his moggy with slickly marketed homogenized abattoir pulp, from animals appallingly reared and slaughtered.

As a result his cats' teeth rapidly accumulate a thick layer of calculus, and the wildlife the brute captures, out of instinct alone and not hunger, is left uneaten to rot, after being tortured slowly to death. A scientist who caused a fraction of this distress to laboratory rats, even with a genuinely noble end in mind, would rightly be pilloried.

---

[67] see Cat Lovers p35

What this means is that there's a vast market for pet dental care aids: dog chews, pet toothbrushes, toothpastes, gum sprays *etc*. Cue the smart-ass American veterinary training video: 'Virtually every routine vaccination can be seen as a marketing opportunity. Suggest the animal is booked in for its teeth to be cleaned, or suggest the client might like to purchase a doggy toothbrush. . . '

So you can make money by selling inappropriate food, and then by selling more stuff to fix the problems this causes. In the meantime there are many people on this planet who don't even have clean drinking water, never mind food, medicine, shelter. . . What a s(l)ick, s(l)ick world we live in!

Performing dental scaling and extraction must be one of the most abysmal jobs a vet has to do. Try to palm 'dentals' off on the nurses if you can. If you do end up doing them, you'll find that the ultrasonic scaler is on the blink, that there isn't a root elevator fine enough to be of any use, and all eleven hacksaw blades choking up the dental kit are blunt and rusted to hell! This means that within a few minutes you'll be sweating and furious, and will attempt to pull multi-rooted teeth without sectioning them, so the roots will break off, and you'll have to dig for them, using inappropriate tools, which will slip and lacerate the gums, and the bleeding will make 'Psycho' look like an expurgated version of 'Five Go Camping', and you'll miss lunch, again.

Time Off

Time off means time off, away from work, not being on call, not being a vet – right? Wrong.

If you're a novice veterinarian you might well be offered accommodation at the practice. What this means, firstly, is that all the other vets will feel free to call upon your services at any time, should they want help with an after-hours call, or if they want an in-patient checked and they can't be bothered getting off their *****! Secondly, if patients are kept in of a night, you won't get much sleep with the cacophonous barking of the canine incarcerates.

Even away from your workplace, work will haunt you, and not just in terms of the smells you'll have difficulty washing off.[68] Every shopping trip becomes a nightmare of dodging clients in supermarket aisles to avoid lengthy discussions of Sheba's forthcoming operation, or how much better/worse Benji is after you took him off steroids.[69]

Well, OK, to be fair, you won't even recognise half the people who approach you, so you can't dodge them. For most of a consultation your eyes are on the animal, so unless a client happens to be particularly fetching, or the opposite, or a frequent contributor to the practice's income, the facial physiognomy will not

---

[68] see Abscesses p11 and Anal Glands p18
[69] see Steroids p127

be etched on your memory. Strangers can walk up to you in the street and say, 'Was it two pills three times a day, or three pills twice a day?' I once managed a 15-minute lunch break, and was sitting in my car in the practice car park, relishing the few minutes away from work, when a client and his wife recognised me and consumed my entire desperately needed 'free' period, discussing their little darling, despite the fact that they had an appointment a few minutes later anyway! And they had the gall to see another vet then, so I was unable to add an OCS.[70] Absolute bastards!

A real downer about being a vet (I mean another real downer!) is that, inevitably, there will be occasions when you will be forced to socialise with other veterinary people. They are unable to talk anything other than shop, with a few exceptions (nurses will, of course, happily talk about diets, celebrities or which brand of chocolates they prefer). Your only recourse will be to drink heavily to dull the pain of it all.[71]

---

[70] Obnoxious Client Surcharge
[71] see Owners' Guide to Vets p109

Vaccinations

When one looks at one's appointment diary one is happy to see it booked up with vaccinations (it's highly unlikely that anything genuinely interesting will come in any given session of consultations, so it might as well be booked up with something so dull and routine that one can put one's brain into neutral, and rest) but there's always a niggling doubt. . .

The first hurdle is that one is supposed to examine the animal. Almost invariably you'll find that kittens in for their first vaccinations have ear mites which will set you behind schedule. Whilst in most other vaccinations all you'll pick up is obesity, anal gland problems and dirty teeth, it is possible to discover any other ailment under the sun at the time of vaccination, and don't expect the owners to give away anything either. Often you'll have vaccinated the animal when they'll say, 'Oh, and he's had severe diarrhoea for the last two days.'

Viral vaccinations are usually a cinch. . . provided, of course, the animal holds still. You only have to stay alert enough not to vaccinate the animal twice, or use the wrong vaccine. It can be a bit of drag explaining the ins and outs of feline leukaemia, so you don't raise the subject, or just hand out a leaflet and send the owner away to read it at home. If you're quick you'll have a couple of minutes to relax before the next appointment, unless you have to make out a duplicate vaccination certificate. . . or unless three animals come through the door although the appointment was for one. . . or unless you have to clip the animal's claws[72] also!

The kennel cough vaccine, or, strictly the vaccine against the commonest bacterial cause of this disease, is an ordeal to administer, as it has to be squirted into the nostrils. Dogs do not enjoy having one of their most sensitive sense organs messed with. You might manage reasonably well the first time a dog comes in for it, if you're quick. Subsequent vaccinations will involve an hysterical struggle in the corner, with vet, dog and owner all losing their tempers. As with nail clipping, it's often best to hand out tranquillisers, and get the owner to dope the dog first.

[72] see Nail Clipping p102

Veterinary Students

Ah, the innocent enthusiasm of these bright-eyed youngsters! (Alright, most of them are bleary-eyed, but the rest holds!) As a veterinarian you'll have to get used to having these naive, impressionable and idealistic apprentices following your every move, as they 'see practice' with you.

If you've forgotten everything you learnt at college (most of it's useless anyway) you might be embarrassed when they ask questions. Some of them will really enjoy interrogating you about what's appeared in the latest edition of JAVMA.[73]

Don't worry. Don't even attempt to discuss the treatment of animals. If you care about the souls of these poor misguided Vets in Practice[74] addicts, just focus on talking them out of continuing their studies.

Stamp on their idealism as hard as you can. Try to save them before it's too late. Show them this book! If they still want to be vets then let them see and do everything. Let them watch consultations with your least convivial clients. Let them squeeze anal glands[75] until their fingers ache. Let them post mortem that stinking cat carcase that the RSPCA thinks might

---

[73] a leading veterinary journal
[74] a television series purportedly documenting the experiences of new graduates
[75] see Anal Glands p18

have been kicked to death. Let them scale as many teeth as they want, and then force them to scale some more. Let them assist with the obese Rottweiler spay – in fact book one in for them to do!

Discuss the ethical nightmare[76] that veterinary science entails. Introduce them to other vets so that they can see how widespread is the dissatisfaction. That'll teach them!

---

[76] see Ethics and Motivation p58

Weather, Water and Being Pissed Off (Or Not)

For non-veterinarians a spell of hot dry weather means a walk in the park, ice cream, and fun. For veterinarians it means an initial lull in cases, then a flood of Parvovirus and dogs with cut paws and bite wounds. A hot summer means that you'll go hoarse repeating basic information on flea treatment.

Additionally, few practices seem to be adequately ventilated or air-conditioned, so chronic heat stress will leave you shattered and with a raging headache at the end of every day.

Cold weather means that you'll be besieged with cases of obese tomcats unable to urinate. Lazy perversions of their wild relatives, these creatures often don't like using litter trays, and Tiddles won't venture outdoors for piddles if he's likely to get the shivers. The unvoided urine sits in the bladder, forming crystals and possibly cultivating bacteria. The resultant slurry blocks up the waterworks entirely, and you'll have to unblock it in the middle of the night. (This will be particularly annoying when you discover that the cat was treated for infectious cystitis a month ago, but the other vet gave it only a few days of antibiotics and failed to suggest any dietary modifications!)

You're a plumber now but don't think you'll get

paid anything near what a real plumber would charge!
First you'll need to drip and anaesthetise the wretched
retentive. This is not easy because Tiddles will be in
agony and will go through the roof (I mean through
your skin!) every time he's touched.

Then you'll need to find the cat catheters – fingers
crossed that the nurses haven't forgotten to re-order
them! Examine your chosen catheter carefully. There
should be a hole in the side of it near the tip. (I once
struggled for a long time to place a catheter only to
discover later that it was a dead-ended dud.) Now use
one hand to exteriorise and stabilise the penis and the
other to insert the catheter. This is darned awkward
because the penis is very small and flabby and col-
lapses when you try to push the tube home. Every
failed attempt means that the opening will be more
bruised and swollen, so things will get progressively
more difficult. . . If you succeed in placing the catheter
you now have to drain and flush the bladder. This can
be very slow and frustrating, because the catheter will
repeatedly block. Once all this has been done, stitch
the catheter in place and for heaven's sake, put a large
bucket collar round the cat's neck or it'll undo all your
work in no time and the next day you'll have to start
from square one!

Rainy weather generally brings about a reduction
in the case load (phew!) but those that do turn up
leave the waiting and consulting rooms looking like
Somme trenches, so muddy does everything become.
The stench of wet dogs, the awful mugginess of the

atmosphere and facefuls of filthy water from Old English Sheepdogs shaking themselves on the consulting room table are not a few of my favourite things!

So is there any weather that is welcome? Any weather when you're away on holiday in another country. Six feet of snow when it's impossible to do home visits[77] and no one can make it to the surgery.

---

[77] see Home Visits p90

X-Rays

Many practices are equipped with archaic X-ray machines of dubious reliability and safety. They fail to have properly shielded X-ray rooms and have a cavalier attitude, to say the least, to staff safety. You may well find that no one will bother to equip you with an X-ray badge (essential to monitor your cumulative exposure to potentially carcinogenic radiation). You might be expected to hold animals for X-rays.

One of the vets in one of the practices I worked in decided to test the so-called protective aprons. He found that he could place the apron on a radiography plate and take an acceptable X-ray picture right through it – it offered no protection whatsoever! Add this to the abandon with which X-rays are taken: 'Oh, we'll just take an X-ray to be sure.' Unfortunately, clients used to vets saying things like this take some persuading that a slight limp is no immediate reason to perform radiography. If the boss finds out you're not taking every opportunity to maximise his profits . . . well, so help you!

Zoonoses

A friend of mine was halfway through a motorway journey of a couple of hundred miles when she started to feel unwell: pounding headache, blurred vision, nausea, weakness. She pulled into a service area and managed to phone for help before she collapsed. She had been injecting a dog a few days previously and had jabbed herself with a needle. She had contracted leptospirosis and was seriously ill for some time.

Zoonoses, or, more correctly, anthropozoonoses, are diseases that one can catch from animals. The most common is ringworm, but nasty infections after being bitten or scratched are neither rare nor trivial.

Other possibilities abound, and include the afore-mentioned leptospirosis, acariasis (mite and tick infestations, such as scabies), anthrax, brucellosis (undulant fever), assorted viral haemorrhagic fevers, helminthiasis (worm infestations), psittacosis, rabies, toxoplasmosis and various gastro-intestinal afflictions.

Vets die from these. In addition to infectious diseases, allergic reactions to animals, pre-operative scrubs, the latex in gloves, or even the powder used to facilitate the donning of these supposedly protective items, make many vets lives miserable. And woe betide you if you should accidentally jab yourself with rabbit VHD vaccine![78]

---

[78] The artery supplying the injected digit will go into spasm and you'll probably ending up losing a finger.

A TYPICAL DAY IN A VET'S LIFE

To get the full flavour of the drudgery of a vet's life you have three options. Firstly, you could read this section. Secondly you could repeatedly select sections at random from the rest of this book (say, 30 times, to simulate a day's work) and re-read them. If you find that the same sections come up several times, then, take my word for it, your boredom at re-reading them will be as nothing to your boredom at actually doing the job! The third option is to go and see practice, and tell the vets to be honest with you about their work and how they feel about it!

Let's start on Monday morning. Your radio alarm clock goes off at 8 am .. You're exhausted as you only got to bed at 3 am after a 2 am recall. This followed a frenetic weekend consulting at three branch practices, with multiple recalls and three home visits. You press the 'snooze' button for another ten minutes in bed.

Breakfast at 8.30 am is interrupted by a nurse buzzing your telephone from the practice downstairs: could you come down a bit early as an MOP[79] has turned up with a badly mangled cat? You curse, and abandon the aforementioned repast. The cat is gasping its last, but you still have to put it down and counsel the MOP, who ran it over. That leaves you five minutes to grab a cup of coffee (essential) and brush your teeth (optional).

You arrive downstairs again at 9.01 am. Two of your

---

[79] member of the public

appointees are waiting already, but Mrs. X is on the phone, wanting to know what's happened to Benji's laboratory tests. You tell the nurse that you'll contact the laboratory and phone her back later.

Your first appointment is supposed to be a routine first vaccination ('Oh, isn't he sweet!'-type nonsense), but the puppy looks stunted to you, and you detect a very loud heart murmur.[80] You suspect a persistent ductus arteriosus, potentially very serious, but you can't be bothered going into all the ins and outs of this at the moment so you tell the client that sometimes murmurs in young puppies are what is technically called 'innocent' and that you will check again in four weeks at the time of the second vaccination.

The second appointment is a Cavalier King Charles Spaniel and fortunately it is just in for its anal glands[81] to be squeezed. It's quite a difficult one and some secretion drops onto the table, and the dog steps on it and smears it everywhere. The smell will linger for the whole day, despite repeated use of an air freshener.

The third case is an adult cat with long-term ear problems.[82] The stench combines unsympathetically with the anal gland odour from the last patient. Unfortunately the batteries of the otoscope/auroscope (if you call it one of these, everyone else in the practice will use the other term, and they'll refuse to understand you, so just use both terms always) are flat, and there are no freshly recharged batteries available, so you have to wait until the other consulting vet has finished using her scope. When this eventually becomes avail-

---

[80] see Heart Failure p88
[81] see Anal Glands p18
[82] see Ears p55

able you are not surprised to discover ear polyps which will probably mean that you'll have to operate, but for now you explain to the owner how to treat the ears medically, to get the inflammation under control, knowing full well that she won't manage. You scrub your hands repeatedly after this consultation but can't get shot of the smell, which has impregnated your inflamed and cracked skin.

The fourth client has brought two cats, three children and a dog. The previous consultations have had to be carried out over the hysterical barking of this undisciplined mutt and the even more hysterical screams of the even more undisciplined children, the older two of which open every cupboard in your consulting room and start playing with the syringes. The mother does nothing and you yourself have to tell them to stop. The middle kid then starts wailing at the unaccustomed admonition and fails to harmonise beautifully with the youngest one who has been caterwauling in mother's arms since entering the practice.

The dog, an extremely boisterous Golden Retriever, is impossible to examine, but fortunately it's just in for a booster vaccination, and a sour-faced nurse manages to stabilise it for a few seconds while you jab it. The first cat has defecated and urinated in its carrying cage, and you have to clean this out, dumping the excrement on top of the growing mound of foulness in your stinking waste bin. The cat's fur is also smeared with ordure, and it takes you a good few minutes to raise its surface hygiene to a tolerably examinable level. Unfortunately the cat then makes a bolt for it and ends up in the back of one of the cupboards which one of the kids has left open. It's now hissing furiously. You decide to leave it there to cool off while you examine the second cat.

This turns out to be a geriatric wreck, barely existing on borrowed time, and now it's the oldest child's turn to scream when you suggest that the skeletal shorthair should be put down.[83] Fortunately the owner agrees to leave it with you. The first cat is quieter now, and you manage to grab it with a towel, having suffered only moderate lacerations to your arms. It's in for a routine vaccination, and, like the dog, you fail to perform a useful examination and are happy just to stick something sharp into it.

While you are completing the vaccination certificates a nurse enters to say that Mrs. X has phoned back again about Benji's results. You are livid, but it's not good form to lose your temper in front of a client so you bite your lower lip, and say, 'But I told her I'd phone her back. I'll be busy consulting for another hour yet!'

The nurse says, 'Yes, but she has to go out now, and she won't be back until late tonight.'

'Well, that isn't really my problem is it? But why don't you take the initiative and phone the laboratory yourself?'

You fail to keep the sarcasm out of your voice, and the nurse slams the door as she leaves. Now she'll go out of her way to make your life miserable for the rest of the week. She's a bitter cow anyway, because her boyfriend treats her like dirt, so the other nurses tell you.

---

[83] Euthanasia, see p61

There follow a couple of genuine routine vaccinations, thank goodness, and then a rabbit with maggots. The owner faints on you (quite common), and you summon the bitter bitch of a nurse to provide a glass of water.

The next case is the one you've been dreading. A really repugnant cat breeder, Mrs. Y, has to be informed that two of her breeding queens are Coronavirus positive.[84] In effect this means that they'll have to be kept isolated from the others until they test clear. She goes through the roof, and implies that you're accusing her of bad husbandry. She is completely irrational.

The receptionist slips you a sympathetic glance as you pick up the card for your next case, fortunately just to have some stitches out, though the owner uses the opportunity to complain about the cost of the operation (a cat spay). You want to say, 'Well, why the hell did you get a cat if you can't afford to have it spayed?' but you bite your tongue. Finally it's time for a tea break, and you gulp your already cold tea down double-quick.

Now it's time for operations: an obese Labrador spay (booked in by the boss who's not working today, the bastard!), two cat spays, three cat castrations, a dog dental and a lump removal. The clippers don't work properly so the nurse has to dismantle them, clean and spray the parts, and reassemble them. This should, of

---

[84] A common group of viruses which can cause anything from mild transient diarrhoea to the horrendous FIP (feline infectious peritonitis) in which the chest and/or abdomen can fill up with purulent fluid or the organs can be invaded by inflammatory cells.

course, have been done the previous day. (As you have learnt by now, the commonest phrase in all veterinary practices is: 'These clippers are useless!')

It's not much of an improvement, and all the animals operated on that day will have severe abrasions as a result. The bitch spay is a nightmare, and you have to call the sour nurse to help you with this, which worsens your relationship even more. Two of the cats go berserk when you try to anaesthetise them and you have to bung them in the crush cage.[85] Some appalling ultra-lowbrow local radio station is being played full-blast by the junior nurses, and the noise level is nerve-shattering.

You have half an hour after operations and before you're due to start afternoon consultations. You've just sat down, about to tuck into your lunchtime sandwich, when the phone-cum-intercom goes off again.

Mrs. Y has decided to have both her Coronavirus positive cats put down, and wants a home visit IMME-DIATELY. She's worth a lot of money to the practice, the partners have stressed to you, so you can't simply refuse. You phone her, and very, very patiently explain yet again that her cats are not necessarily going to develop any illness at all, and may well be entirely virus-free in the near future. There's no need to put them down. Unfortunately that's your lunch-break over.

The morning was quiet compared to the afternoon. You squeeze six pairs of anal glands, diagnose three

---

[85] An essential item of veterinary equipment that would not look out of place in a bondage parlour. I leave it to your imagination.

cases of mammary cancer, discover one retained testicle, detect three cases of ear mites, treat two cats with abscesses, remove 56 stitches, recommend five dentals, discuss fleas and obesity until you're so fatigued that you can't even speak clearly, and inject 22 millilitres of vaccine, 82 ml of antibiotics, and 10 ml of corticosteroids, on top of dispensing a total of 342 tablets, five packets of rehydration salts, 250 ml of kaolin and pectin and eight wormers of various sorts.

Between the afternoon and evening sessions you have to go a home visit, which turns out to be a complete waste of time (nothing wrong with the animal, but the owner is crazy).

The evening consultation session makes the afternoon's look like a rest cure. By the time you finish it's 8.20 pm. The evil bitch-troll of a nurse has left you a note to say that Mrs. X's dog's blood samples were never received by the laboratory – had you perhaps forgotten to send them? No, you'd delegated that task to. . . ? You can't bloody remember and you no longer give a damn. You've got to get away from the wretched place and get p*ssed, never mind that you're exhausted! You phone a non-veterinary friend and hit the pub.

You stagger back home around midnight to notice the lights on downstairs. It's one of your bosses on call tonight. 'Good,' you think to yourself, 'It's about bloody time that he did some work!' You stumble upstairs to bed. At 2 am you awake for a call of nature, and find you have an appalling headache. You try to sleep but can't. It's not only your headache, it's also the in-patients barking in hell below. You toss and curse for a while, and then pull on some clothes and totter downstairs. Unfortunately, when you get down there all five dogs are silent.

You go upstairs again, and the barking recommences. This time you are more than angry. You stomp downstairs again, and inject every dog with a high dose of tranquilliser, all but one. This one is fast asleep. It's the dog you'd spayed earlier, and the cage notes tell you that the partner was recalled as it haemorrhaged extensively. In fact he was busy re-operating on this when you got back from the pub. Now you can't sleep because you feel so guilty and inadequate. You doze off eventually at 5.34 am. Ah, yes, the end to a typical day in the life of a recent graduate. So satisfying, so fulfilling. Great career choice.

Postscript:
Come the next day's consultations you have such a dreadful hangover that you have to excuse yourself frequently to go and throw up. You consider injecting yourself with something. . .

ADVICE FOR WOULD-BE VETERINARIANS

Being a modern veterinary practitioner generally bears little similarity to the delightful bucolic image the profession seems to have. I fail to understand what satisfaction small animal veterinarians can get from their jobs, assuming they are at all idealistic or think about the issues, and, indeed I've met few vets who admit to being satisfied.

Nonetheless, let's assume that having read this book, and having discussed and verified its contents with practising vets, you are still determined to become one. Are you perhaps out to become a money-grabbing bastard of a partner, or are you a masochist? Let's assume it's for some other reason, though I know not what it could be. In that case I have some advice:

1) Preferably use your veterinary degree as a springboard from which to explore something else. Go into industry or research. If you can face further study then taking an M.B.A. or an M.Sc. will open more doors for you. A Ph.D. takes longer and the rewards might not be commensurate with the effort, although it is nice to be able to correct people who call you Miss/Ms/Mrs/Mr!

2) If you decide to enter practice then try to work part-time or do locums. You will have a lot more time

to do other things, and you won't get bored or frustrated half as quickly. Locums are relatively well-paid, and you have the additional interest of going to new places and meeting new people. If you are settled (*i.e.* with a house and family), then as long as you live within a reasonable distance of major urban areas (*e.g.* London, or in the Manchester-Warrington-Liverpool area) you should be able to find a steady supply of jobs within commuting distance.

3) If you do take a 'permanent' job, choose it very, very carefully. By all means consider the salary, but no amount of money will make up for being worked into the ground, or not getting on with your colleagues. Try to contact the vet you are replacing, or failing that try to speak privately to another assistant veterinarian, and ask why that person is leaving. Ask about the hours and the other personnel. Remember, what the boss tells you and what actually happens are two different things. There's little point in having plenty of time off if you're too exhausted to use it. For example, if it's an eight-vet practice, with a one-in-eight after-hours rota, then you can be sure that being on call will be a nightmare. It'll take you days to recover, and the anticipatory stress will ruin the period before your duty night or weekend. Other things to consider are what your social life will be like, how far it is to the nearest bright lights, and if there are facilities nearby for you to exercise your hobbies, whatever they may be. If you don't have any, get some quick! Do not expect being a vet to fulfil you!

You have been warned!

SUGGESTIONS FOR THE IMPROVEMENT OF THE VETERINARY PROFESSION

Here are a few ideas I had when I was sober:

1) There's little point selecting people on academic ability when the job seldom requires this but does demand tremendous 'people skills' and patience. However, research has shown, time and time again, that interviewing is a very poor way of selecting people. Prospective veterinary students should undergo a more rigorous assessment of their emotional stability and social skills. (I admit that I would probably have failed such an assessment, but then so would many other vets out there!) Once selected, veterinary students ought to be taught the principles of personnel and business management. At the very least they should learn that carrots are far more effective management tools than sticks. Needless to say, the psychological aspects of the job should be emphasised.

2) To some extent an alternative to the above would be to give nurses a great deal more responsibility. This would reduce the requirement for veterinary surgeons, as well as improve the quality of the professional lives of both nurses and vets. There's no point training people for five or more years and then getting them to spend 95 % of their time on the mundane drudgery

described in this book. It ought to be possible to devise a simple step-by-step manual/key to cover routine consulting, vaccinations and the like, which could be followed by veterinary nurses. Any condition which turned out not to be satisfactorily diagnosed and treated by such a simple manual, or required the prescription of more than a limited list of basic drugs, would then have to be referred to a vet. Clients could always have the option of requesting a veterinarian's attentions initially. This would, of course, be more expensive!

3) Lay down and enforce rules regarding the number of hours assistant veterinarians, nurses and receptionists can be expected to work on both a daily and a weekly basis. Exhausted people do not work efficiently.

4) Vets and veterinary nurses should be encouraged to join a trade union.

FURTHER SUGGESTIONS FOR THE IMPROVEMENT OF THE PROFESSION

Before being admitted to veterinary college, prospective veterinary students should have to pass an exam on the contents of this book. The consequence would be a vastly reduced number of applicants and a proper enquiry into this seriously troubled profession. The publicity would encourage pet owners and breeders, and members of the public in general, to read the book also, and so confront the irrationality of many of their attitudes to pets and vets.

Pet ownership would be considerably reduced, freeing money to go to charities supporting broken-down vets and to dealing with other issues of international concern such as littering, global warming, the unfairness of international trade, the scandal of the government-backed arms trade, the outrage of Guantanamo Bay, the provision of clean drinking water, vaccination, the scourges of AIDS and malaria, the appalling state of education (with teachers being treated abysmally by unscrupulous tabloid-driven politicians) such that no one knows how to use an apostrophe and even Lynne Truss uses redundancies like 'work colleagues' *etc.*, *etc.*

Animal rights activists would divert their attention

155

from the relatively trivial issues of laboratory animals and fox-hunting to focus on the mass abuse constituted by much modern agriculture. So-called 'animal lovers' who happily eat meat produced under conditions of dreadful cruelty, and feed such meat to their carnivorous pets, would not replace the latter, would eat less meat themselves, and only consume such that had been humanely produced. With less production of inefficient animal protein, existing resources would feed more people, energy wastage being considerably reduced.

With an increased awareness of the plight of fellow human beings, and the shared goal of making the world a better place, people would be less focussed on material goods as they developed more rewarding relationships with members of their own species. Concomitantly, the 'need' for people-substitute pets would decline, further reducing the pet population as the virtuous circle accelerated.

With fewer pets and farm animals there would be less of a need for vets, so the decline in veterinary applicants would not matter, and those who applied for the course despite having read this book, would be well aware of what lay in store for them. Fewer people would be needed to staff the helplines for stressed/alcoholic/druggie vets.

We will know that the world has finally been saved when the veterinary profession is represented by only a handful of balanced and competent individuals, who work sensible hours, have both time and energy for other interests and activities, and who earn a decent living without lying, bullying and exploiting their employees. Such happy men and women would be treated with respect by their intelligent and informed clients, and paid on time!

Ha bloody ha! Dream on. I'm hitting the pub now. And if anyone asks me about his mutt's itchy backside he can go to hell!

Are you looking at me? I asked you a question! Are you looking at me?

Josh Artmeier is a lover of
humans and animals and is a vet.
He has worked from the south of
England to the north of Scotland,
as well as in Wales.

Share your views with Josh at
www.myspace.com/pethates